The Mode of Info

The Mode of Information

Poststructuralism and Social Context

Mark Poster

Polity Press

First published 1990 by Polity Press in association with Basil Blackwell

Editorial office:
Polity Press, 65 Bridge Street,
Cambridge CB2 1UR, UK

Marketing and production:
Basil Blackwell Ltd
108 Cowley Road, Oxford OX4 1JF

ISBN 0 7456 0326 2
ISBN 0 7456 0327 0 (pbk)

British Library Cataloguing in Publication Data

A CIP catalogue record for this book is available from the British Library.

Typeset in 10½ on 12 pt Sabon
by Photo·graphics, Honiton, Devon
Printed in Great Britain by T.J. Press (Padstow) Ltd, Padstow, Cornwall.

Contents

Acknowledgements

The position I develop in this book evolved over a period of several years. During that time many colleagues and friends participated in that process by their comments, suggestions, criticisms, encouragements, warnings. I thank the following people for that help and for reading various parts of the manuscript: David Carroll, Andrew Feenberg, Rob Kling, Tania Modleski, Leslie Rabine, John Rowe, Gabriele Schwab, Martin Schwab, Miriam Silverberg, Jonathan Wiener. Robert Sieber helped me with the research on the discipline of Computer Science that is discussed in chapter 5. In the course of presenting the material in this book at various institutions I received helpful responses from many persons. For their interest and concern I thank them. I benefited greatly, as I have for the past decade, from the work of the Critical Theory Institute at the University of California, Irvine, and this not only by its financial support but also by the responses to my work by its members. A University of California President's Research Fellowship in the Humanities allowed me the time to bring this work to its conclusion. Students in the History Department and the Emphasis in Critical Theory at the University of California, Irvine were helpful in their skepticism, enthusiasm or critique of my ideas. Part of the introduction is appearing in the journal *October*, 54 (Winter 1990) as "Words without Things: The Mode of Information." Part of chapter 3 appeared in *Discourse*, 12(2) (Spring–Summer 1990) as "Foucault and Data Bases." An early version of part of chapter 4 will appear in "The Subject of the Computer: Derrida and Electronic Writing," in José Lambert, ed., *Literature and Technology* (Baltimore: Johns Hopkins University Press, forthcoming).

Introduction

Words without Things

A relatively thinly populated country, with well-developed means of communication, has a denser population than a more numerously populated country, with a badly-developed means of communication; and in this sense the Northern States of the American Union, for instance, are more thickly populated than India.

Karl Marx, *Capital*

An increasing segment of communications is mediated by electronic devices. People watch television, make phone calls, listen to the radio, go to the movies, use computers, fax machines, VCRs and stereos. Such communications occur in every institution and in every social group. Politics, work, consumption, the family, the military, the church, education, leisure activities – in varying degrees all employ electronic mechanisms in their communications. In each instance, symbols are exchanged, messages are sent and received, information is retrieved just as they have been since human beings began using language. And yet something has changed as well. Electronic communications are new language experiences in part by virtue of electrification. But how are they different from ordinary speech and writing? And what is the significance of this difference? This book explores these differences and in particular considers various theoretical perspectives that might be useful for opening new interpretive strategies for critical social theory in relation to these differences.

Some observers argue that the introduction of electronic devices makes no substantial difference in the nature or consequence of a communication. The politician who speaks in a TV ad campaign still attempts to gain votes according to the rules of constitutional democracy. The worker who uses a computer to control an assembly process or type a letter is paid for his or her labor as in the past according to the contract of employment. The consumer who watches a TV merely gains information about products that might be bought in a store, much like reading a newspaper. The soldier who uses a computer to guide a projectile to its target, like the archer who visually aims his arrow, is practicing the art of destroying the enemy. The electronic device simply increases the efficiency of the communication in question. From this perspective language appears as a tool for the purposes of acting human subjects, clearly subordinate in importance to the positional intentions of individuals in determinate institutional frameworks.

Nor do electronic devices nullify the theories that explain the nature of communications. To a Marxist, new communications devices fall within the thesis of the class struggle: increased access to information occurs differentially in relation to one's position in the class structure. To neoMarxists, electronic media reinforce the culture industry, heightening the hegemonic force of ideology. To an economist, the laws of the market determine who shall use a computer, who shall advertise on television, who shall have their songs broadcast to radio receivers. To a Weberian, electronic communications increase the differentiation of society into subsystems and promote the power of bureaucracy. To a liberal they are subject to the contest for power among pluralist factions. Even for technological determinists, nothing is new: electronic media confirm the progress of the proliferation of machines that alleviate toil and subordinate nature to the wishes of mankind. Regardless of one's theoretical perspective, the conclusion appears incontrovertible that with the introduction of electronically mediated communication nothing basic has changed.

These perspectives all recognize and account for one sort of modification introduced by electronic communications: the exchange of symbols between human beings is now far less subject to constraints of space and time. In principle, information is now instantly available all over the globe and may be stored and retrieved as long as electricity is available. Time and space no longer restrict the exchange of information. McLuhan's "global village" is technically feasible and as such has important consequences that call into question the adequacy of existing theories and positions. The electronic reproduction of scenes from Vietnam into American homes in the late 1960s had stunning impact on politics. The capture of a government television station by the Philippine rebels in 1985 and their subsequent broadcasts reassuring the population of their success materially affected the fate of the Marcos regime. The recent introduction of direct retailing on television portends a revolution in the marketing practices of consumer goods. The apprehension of suspected criminals by clues provided through the computer analysis of fingerprints affords a new level of information to law enforcement agencies. The prospect of instant universal information, introduced by electronic media, clearly has profound effects on society, the extent of which are still to be determined. But the conquest of space and time by electronic media augurs more for institutions and for theory than a mere retuning of practices and ideas to new communicational frequencies.

The new level of interconnectivity afforded by electronic media, for instance, heightens the fragility of social networks. Take the example of computer networks at research facilities. Early in November 1988, newspapers reported that a network (ARPAnet) of military, corporate and university computers, some 6,000 across the country, were "infected by a virus" and consequently rendered dysfunctional.[1] A "virus" is a small "program" or set of commands that attaches itself to other programs or files so that it reproduces itself while also executing its routines. The virus spreads both within a computer and from one computer to another as files or messages are transmitted between them. The virus also carries out commands, which vary from the innocuous "Display 'Gotcha!' on the screen" to the disastrous "Delete all files on the hard disk." In November, the virus in question tied up the computers' memory by simply reproducing itself *ad infinitum*. The shut down of ARPAnet was costly and frustrating to users. Even though no files were damaged, no information lost, and no known crime committed, the FBI was called in to locate the perpetrator.

A virus is an agent that spreads disease among living organisms. The metaphorical application of the term to computers underscores the likeness of computer networks to living bodies: computers are so profoundly interconnected that they may behave like parts of a body. Machines that are mechanically interconnected normally are unable to transmit physical forces to other machines, thereby remaining unaffected by malfunctions at other points in a chain. Computers that are informationally connected are, like living bodies, able to pass complex instructions to one another, instructions that may disable the entire computer network. With more and more institutions increasingly connected by computer networks and dependent upon them for their functioning, society has spawned electronic, informational "bodies" which, like human communities, are subject to "epidemics." At a time when the AIDS virus threatens the human community, other "viruses" threaten the society of computers. If the AIDS virus is transmitted by sexual contact, the computer virus, in the case of ARPAnet, was initiated in a psychosexual Oedipal context: the author of the virus is a graduate student at Cornell University whose father is a computer security consultant. Cybernoanalysis and psychoanalysis may apparently become related fields. But computer viruses are quite common and are increasing in frequency. In January and February 1989 a combined total of 3,000 viruses were reported.[2] Instead of a Freudian Oedipal drama, viruses might be seen as a new form of resistance against those who control computerized information.

At quite another level, reports are spreading that computer monitors, indeed the entire electronic network, affect the body of the user at the profound level of altering DNA.[3] If the metaphor of the virus suggests that networks of computers form a new social body, the possible radiation effects of working with computer monitors suggests the strong link between computer and computer user. A symbiotic merger between human and machine might literally be occurring, one that threatens the stability of our sense of the boundary of the human body in the world. What may be happening is that human beings create computers and then computers create a new species of humans. This theme has been anticipated in numerous films (such as *Robocop*) and science fiction stories (in particular those of Philip K. Dick). These speculations must not divert us from the more direct problem at hand though they may lead in fruitful directions.

The speed at which computer viruses spread spotlights the new fragility of society in the age of the mode of information. Very little time elapsed between the initial transmission of the virus to the shutdown of the entire network. Similarly in the stock market collapse of October 1987 news from New York passed instantly to London and Tokyo and their reactions passed back to New York just as quickly. Distance provided no buffer between remote points that might allow time for reactions to be deliberated. Financial panic at one center spread to the other centers as quickly as the sense of danger spreads among a herd of animals. The report of the event in the *New York Times* noticed the impact of computers on the slide in stock prices.[4] The communications network that ties the world's financial hubs together for better access to information also threatens them with instant economic collapse. Thus the simple, utilitarian advantage of efficient language transmission becomes, through increased speed alone, a new social phenomenon, as quantity "dialectically" transmutes into quality. And this social phenomenon urges, perhaps as never before, careful attention to and examination of the linguistic dimension of culture.

Some analysts recognize that the study of electronic communication requires more than attention to new technologies or machines and signifies more than progressive increases in the efficiency of symbolic exchanges. In one such study, Carolyn Marvin argues that the history of electronic communication "is less the evolution of technical efficiencies in communication than a series of arenas for negotiating issues crucial to the conduct of social life; among them, who is inside and outside, who may speak, who may not, and who has authority and may be believed."[5] She is able to demonstrate, for example, that the introduction of the telephone did more than enable people to communicate over long distances: it threatened existing class relations by extending the boundary of who may speak to whom; it also altered modes of courtship and possibilities of romance. Similarly the introduction of the electric light bulb seriously changed mass leisure and culture: for instance, night-time spectator sports, with their deep impact on mass culture, were creatures of the light bulb.[6] Clearly then electronic communication opens major social questions.

Marvin theorizes her perspective on electronic communication as follows: New technologies "intended to streamline, simplify, or otherwise enhance the conduct of familiar social routines may so reorganize them that they become new events."[7] With this thematic she recognizes the role of cultural and social forms in shaping new communications patterns at the point of technological innovation, but she does not question some of the broader, theoretical implications of these changes. In order to discern "new events" or new communications one must problematize the nature of communications in modern society by retheorizing the relation between action and language, behavior and belief, material reality and culture. Although the culturalist perspective enacted in analyses such as Marvin's represents an important advance in the study of communications, it does not go far enough in questioning dominant theoretical and disciplinary paradigms in relation to the new communicational forms.

An adequate account of electronic communications requires a theory that is able to decode the linguistic dimension of the new forms of social interaction. As a step toward that end I am offering the concept of the mode of information. The term "the mode of information" plays upon Marx's theory of the mode of production. In *The German Ideology* and elsewhere Marx invokes the concept of the mode of production in two ways: (1) as a historical category which divides and periodizes the past according to variations in the mode of production (differing combinations of means and relations of production); (2) as a metaphor for the capitalist epoch which privileges economic activity as, in Althusser's phrase, "the determination in the last instance." By mode of information I similarly suggest that history may be periodized by variations in the structure in this case of symbolic exchange, but also that the current culture gives a certain fetishistic importance to "information."

Every age employs forms of symbolic exchange which contain internal and external structures, means and relations of signification. Stages in the mode of information may be tentatively designated as follows: face-to-face, orally mediated exchange; written exchanges mediated by print; and electronically mediated exchange. If the first stage is characterized by symbolic correspondences, and the second stage is characterized by the representation of signs, the third is characterized by informational simulations. In the first, oral stage the self is constituted as a position of enunciation through its embeddedness in a totality of face-to-face relations. In the second, print stage the self is constructed as an agent centered in rational/ imaginary autonomy. In the third, electronic stage the self is decentered, dispersed, and multiplied in continuous instability.

In each stage the relation of language and society, idea and action, self and other is different. Some of these differences are discussed in chapter 3. Here I want to stress that the stages are not "real," not "found" in the documents of each epoch, but imposed by the theory as a necessary step in the process of attaining knowledge. In this sense the stages are not sequential but coterminous in the present. They are not consecutive also since elements of each are at least implicit in the others. The logical status of the concept of the mode of information is both historical and transcendental. In that sense the latest stage is not the privileged, dialectical resolution of previous developments. In one sense, however, a sense that Marx anticipated, the current configuration constitutes a necessary totalization of earlier developments: that is, one cannot but see earlier developments from the situation of the present. The anatomy of the mode of electronic information, to paraphrase Marx, necessarily sheds new light on the anatomy of oral and print modes of information. The danger that must be avoided in Marx's formulation is progressivism. I prefer to consider the present age as simply an unavoidable context of discursive totalization, not as an ontological realization of a process of development.

If the stages prove to have heuristic value they will become integrated into the repertoire of standpoints through which we understand our past and in that sense they are "historical." As Marx notes in *The German Ideology*, the test of any theory is determined in empirical studies informed by its concepts. In this spirit, my book is to be taken above all as an attempt to suggest the value of poststructuralist theory to the history of communications, to promote a new direction of research in that field, and therefore to be considered one theme in what Foucault called the history of the present.

For now I want to mention some peculiarities of the term "information" and suggest that it takes on a special valence in the third stage. In a sense all signs are now considered information, as in cybernetics and often in popular parlance, where "information" is contrasted with "noise" or non-meaning. Information has become a privileged term in our culture. TV ads for information services warn consumers and corporate executives alike that they or their children will fall behind in the race for success if they do not keep up with current information. Information is presented as the key to contemporary living and society is divided between the information rich and the information poor. The "informed" individual is a new social ideal, particularly for the middle class, a group to which in the United States everyone but the homeless claims to belong. The term "information" in the title then evokes a certain feature of the new cultural conjuncture that must be treated with suspicion.

With that warning in mind, I want to suggest some of the chief areas of concern in the study of the mode of information. It must include a study of the forms of information storage and retrieval, from cave paintings and clay tablets to computer databases and communications satellites. Each method of preserving and transmitting information profoundly intervenes in the network of relationships that constitute a society. After the population attains a certain size, for example, government cannot expand without written records. Human messengers, relying only upon their memory, impose a severe limit on the power of the state. Only so much of resources can be allocated to communication before military and economic sectors begin to suffer. Cheap, reliable, durable communication is a necessity of empire.

It is only a little farfetched to assert that World War One might have been avoided if Emperor Franz Joseph and Kaiser Wilhelm II had communicated by telephone or modem instead of by telegraph. After the assassination of the Austrian Archduke, the German and Austrian governments had been urgently exchanging messages concerning their response to news of Russian mobilizations. With the limitations of the telegraph, the Kaiser's message to the Emperor to the effect that Germany would prefer not to back up an Austrian attack on Serbia was received too late to prevent war – it came a couple of hours after the attack already had begun.[8] Today the populace fears total annihilation through nuclear holocaust which looms only more probable as a result of the formidable speed of communication systems. In the same vein, the depth and importance of communications media is evident when it is realized that contemporary mass society in its present form is inconceivable without the printing press.[9] Political events, forms of community, economic systems all are coordinated with communication media. If the windmill is associated with feudalism and the steam engine capitalism, again to paraphase Marx, similarly electronic communications, I suggest, may be associated with the mode of information. The extent to which communication is restricted by time and space governs, with striking force, the shape society may take.

While the study of the temporal and spatial distanciation of communication is important to the concept of the mode of information[10] the heart of the matter lies elsewhere. For the issue of communicational *efficiency*, which is at stake in the above discussion, does not raise the basic question of the *configuration* of information exchange, or what I call the wrapping of language. Unless traditional assumptions about the nature of society and the theory that would comprehend it are called into question, the study of communicational distanciation remains only an addendum, however important, to established points of view. If communication only facilitates or impedes other activities it has no independent consequences. In that case, there is little justification for a new theoretical initiative such as the mode of information. But I shall argue otherwise: that the configuration of communication in any given society is an analytically autonomous realm of experience, one that is worthy of study in its own right. Furthermore, in the twentieth century the rapid introduction of new communicational modes constitutes a pressing field for theoretical development and empirical investigation. What is at stake are new language formations that alter significantly the network of social relations, that restructure those relations and the subjects they constitute.

The example of music reproduction illustrates the way electronic mediation changes the language situation. A coterie of audiophiles strives to produce in their homes an exact copy of original musical performances.[11] Audiophiles maintain that certain recordings contain in their grooves all the information needed to accomplish a miracle of sound technology: the illusion that the listener is there at the live performance of the music. For this magic to occur everything must be just right. Only a handful of recordings qualify for this purpose: a select few by RCA (those with shaded dogs on the label), some from Mercury issued during the late 1950s and early 1960s, and a handful produced by EMI from the 1960s and early 1970s. The stereo components must be carefully selected and matched for a perfect balance of sound reproducing abilities. Even the cables connecting the components are critical. The room itself is also a component since its qualities of sound reflection and absorption affect what the listener hears. Under the right circumstances, audiophiles insist, the listener comes very close to hearing in the home what a person in the concert hall would have heard when the piece being played on the turntable was originally performed. In this case, audiophiles are regarding musical information or language as a neutral medium of artistic expression. In its electronically mediated form, they assume, musical information may be reproduced without alteration. Information as representation here achieves its apotheosis.

The case of recorded rock music presents a quite different configuration of language. Many studio recordings of rock are from the outset structured for reproduction in the home. Most often no original performance exists. Instead each musician is taped on a separate "track;" musicians in some cases actually play the music in different cities and some of the tracks, especially the percussion, may be taped from a synthesizer, without any "performance." An engineer combines the discrete "tracks" into a master tape which constitutes the "original." In doing so, the engineer introduces acute changes: each track is adjusted for amplitude and frequency response or tonal balance. In addition instruments are "repositioned" in the recording within the stereo soundfield, assuming the speakers are properly placed about six feet apart squarely facing the listener. The drums for example are often balanced to appear to emerge alternatively with each beat from the left and right speaker so that the drummer seems to be situated across the spread of the room. The performance that the consumer hears when the recording is played is not a copy of an original but is a simulacrum, a copy that has no original. These rock performances exist *only in their reproduction*. Electronic mediation, in this case, produces millions of copies of musical information that was never performed in the usual sense of the term. Many other examples could be given of information systems which produce simulacra.

Electronic mediation complicates the transmission of language and subverts the subject who would limit language to the role of a simple medium of expression. In the case of the audiophile, the effort to achieve an exact musical reproduction quickly goes beyond the listener's intention. Striving to extract more and more information from the grooves of the vinyl disk, the audiophile soon finds him- or herself hearing *more* than the listener at the original performance. The audiophile claims to discern the space around each instrument, the voices of each instrumental group in complex orchestral passages (such as the violas or second violins), individual singers in choruses, and so forth. While the aim of choruses, for example, is to blend voices into unified waves of sound, the audiophile, aided by expensive stereo gear that resolves complex sounds into their discrete parts, claims to discern individual voices within the ensemble, hearing, through electronic mediation, more "information" than was audible to a listener at the original performance. The obsession to recapture the musical language of the past slides into the production of a new manifold of information. To copy an original means, in the mode of information, to create simulacra.

For many audiophiles what began as a simple quest for musical enjoyment in the home soon becomes an extensive, multifarious quest for a perfect stereo system. More and more time, care and money is invested in the medium of sound reproduction; more and more effort is expended to control the listening environment. Even the electricity coming into the house is suspect as a possible source of distortion: a "line conditioner" must be installed "to decontaminate" the electric current and regulate the voltage more precisely than the company delivering that electricity thinks necessary. As much as possible, the listening room is isolated from the exterior world, reducing the decibel level of ambient street noise. In some cases, the foundation of the room is reinforced and the walls are altered by the installation of a combination of reflective and damping materials to achieve perfect acoustic properties. The body of the audiophile, seated equidistant between two speakers, becomes part of an ideal microworld, an auditory Utopia in which subject and object, listener and room, merge in an identity of blissful sound.

Or so the audiophile dreams. In actuality, desire continuously escapes fulfillment as improvements continuously suggest themselves, intrusions by friends and family members disrupt listening sessions, and imperfections in the system are recognized. The electronic mediation of musical information subverts the autonomous, rational subject for whom language is a direct translation of reality, instantiating instead an infinite play of mirror reflections, an abyss of indeterminate exchanges between subject and object in which the real and the fictional, the outside and the inside, the true and the false oscillate in an ambiguous shimmer of codes, languages, communications. In this world, the subject has no anchor, no fixed place, no point of perspective, no discreet center, no clear boundary. When Foucault wrote in *The Order of Things* that "man" is dead[12] he registered the disorientation of the subject in the mode of information. In electronically mediated communications, subjects now float, suspended between points of objectivity, being constituted and reconstituted in different configurations in relation to the discursive arrangement of the occasion.

In this study I take from poststructuralists the theme that subjects are constituted in acts and structures of communication. I investigate the way changes in communication patterns involve changes in the subject. Changes in the configuration or wrapping of language alters the way the subject processes signs into meanings, that sensitive point of cultural production. The shift from oral and print wrapped language to electronically wrapped language thus reconfigures the subject's relation to the world. If I am successful in demonstrating the effects of electronically mediated communication on the subject the further need will also be apparent to theorize the field of the social, to call into question basic, foundational assumptions of critical social theory and more generally those of the social sciences.

In this book I also hope to contribute to a reconstruction of critical social theory by bringing poststructuralist theory to bear on the phenomena of electronically mediated communication. I hope to demonstrate that new forms of language wrapping are imposing significant changes in the social field, and that poststructuralist theory offers a uniquely appropriate strategy of interpretation in relation to these new phenomena. Conversely I hope also to show the ways in which electronically mediated communication becomes a social context for poststructuralist theory; that turning a poststructuralist gaze upon these social phenomena introduces a feedback effect on that theory, compelling a recalibration of its interpretive habits in important ways.

The first obstacle to the constitution of the field of the mode of information is theoretical. I refer to the tendency among social theorists to objectify meanings, to limit words to single meanings, and to treat language as a transparent tool for action. As an intellectual historian I trace the problem back to its origins. Social theory arose in a Cartesian culture of distinct objects and subjects, in a dualist metaphysics of extended things and minds.[13] In this theoretical context, the social scientist is constituted as a knowing subject separate from his or her object of study, one who enunciates univocal words to define an objective social field distinct from himself or herself. The discourse of social theory is structured as a direct representation of the mind of the social theorist. Within the constituted social field, by contrast, language is presumed to exist at a different level from theory but one that remains univocal. The everyday world of language (opinions, attitudes, ideas and ideology) is also distinct from the world of action, a separate register that may be out of phase with the register of action. Still social scientists regard the social level of discourse, like the discourse of theory, as representing the mind of the individual. In this theoretical context, language is nothing more than a transparent mediation, a representation of consciousness in writing or speech. Within this theoretical economy, electronic communications simply increase the representational power of language by reducing the temporal and spatial distancing of meaning.

Today however the representational character of language is especially fragile and problematic. In sphere after sphere of daily life, the relation of word and thing is complicated by the loss of the referent. Consider for a moment the example of money as a representational sign.[14] At one time it denoted rare, precious metals that were coined by the state and therefore functioned as legal tender. Gold, for example, both functioned as a medium of exchange and was considered valuable in itself. The referent was a stable ground of the word. A correspondence existed between the representational function of gold as a medium of exchange and its specific character as a scarce commodity. The sign "money" represented the thing "gold" with little ambiguity. Money then came to designate bank notes which represented coined precious metals stored in fortified government depositories, but were not precious in themselves since they could be printed in great quantities. The *correspondence* between word and thing was dropped in favor of a relation of *representation*. Later, checks, representing deposits of bank notes, came to serve as money and, being more easily printed than bank notes, were even less precious in themselves. At present bank cards are replacing checks, representing not deposits of bank notes, but electronic information in databases, which in turn are representations of deposits of bank notes. The word "money" now refers to a configuration of oxides on a tape stored in the computer department of a bank. The connection between the oxides and the function of exchange medium is arbitrary, revealing its socially constituted character, and the representational aspect of "money" is sustained through language, through configurations of language, its referent being remote and difficult to discern. The case of "money" illustrates the great elasticity of representational language, the way words can refer to things that are at a very great remove from them, but also to the limits of that elasticity. The next step in linguistic change is the formation of simulacra.

The function of representation comes to grief when words lose their connection with things and come to stand in the place of things, in short, when language represents itself. The complex linguistic worlds of the media, the computer and the databases it can access, the surveillance capabilities of the state and the corporation, and finally, the discourses of science, are each realms in which the representational function of language has been placed in question by different communicational patterns each of which shift to the forefront the self-referential aspect of language. In the pages that follow, a chapter shall be devoted to each of these four new "languages." In each case, the language in question is constituted as an intelligible field with a unique pattern of wrapping, whose power derives not so much from representing something else but from its internal, linguistic structure. While this feature of language is always present in its use, today increasingly meaning is sustained through mechanisms of self-referentiality and the non-linguistic thing, the referent, fades into obscurity, playing less and less of a role in the delicate process of sustaining cultural meanings. In such a cultural context the categories of objectivist social science force a premature closure of knowledge, reducing the ambivalent complexity of the mode of information to the "rationality" of language as a tool for action.

Some social critics complain that the increase in informational language by itself, in such areas as the media, science, the computer, and state and corporate surveillance, undermines the representational function. Recognizing the novelty of so vast a spread of nonrepresentational language, one important theorist, Fredric Jameson, laments: "Unfortunately, no society has ever been quite so mystified in quite so many ways as our own, saturated as it is with messages and information, the very vehicle of mystification. . . ."[15] Language, Jameson suggests, is not a tool for action when its proliferation leads to stultifying confusion. The multiplication of messages, for him, undermines the ability of the brain selectively to discriminate meaning from noise. So impressed is another critic with the recent information explosion that he makes it a new basis for historical periodization. Richard Terdiman writes: "In a world saturated by discourse, language itself becomes contested terrain. I will argue that such saturation is the cultural *differentia specifica* distinguishing the modern period from earlier formations."[16] A full study of the concept of the mode of information requires an assessment of the impact of the mass of self-referential information that confronts the individual. This investigation might provide one measure of the instability of the rational individual or centered subject whose imagined autonomy is associated with a capacity to link sign and referent, word and thing, in short, a representational functioning of language.

The crisis of representation derives, I suggest, not only from the information explosion noted by Jameson and Terdiman, but also from the new communicational structures in which that information circulates. Beyond a certain point, increased distance between addressor and addressee allows a reconfiguration of the relation between emitter and receiver, between the message and its context, between the receiver/subject and representations of him or herself. These reconfigurations, which I call wrappings of language, in turn impose a new relation between science and power, between the state and the individual, between the individual and the community, between *autho*rity and law, between family members, between the consumer and the retailer. In sum the solid institutional routines that have characterized modern society for some two hundred years are being shaken by the earthquake of electronically mediated communication and recomposed into new routines whose outlines are as yet by no means clear.

While to some extent language is a tool for intentional action, and as such must be accounted for within the theory of the mode of information, language has another, very different, capacity: it is a figurative, structuring power that constitutes the subject who speaks as well as the one that is spoken to. Electronically mediated communication has compelling effects at this level of language. By distancing the relation of speaking body to listening body, by abstracting from the connection between the reader or writer and the palpable materiality of the printed or handwritten text, electronically mediated communication upsets the relation of the subject to the symbols it emits or receives and reconstitutes this relation in drastically new shapes. For the subject in electronically mediated communication, the object tends to become not the material world as represented in language but the flow of signifiers itself. In the mode of information it becomes increasingly difficult, or even pointless, for the subject to distinguish a "real" existing "behind" the flow of signifiers, and as a consequence social life in part becomes a practice of positioning subjects to receive and interpret messages.

Marshall McLuhan's axiom that "the medium is the message" points in the direction of the mode of information but does not go far enough. By focusing on the "sensorium" of the receiving subject he preserves the subject as a perceiving, not an interpreting being. He continues the tradition of Lockean epistemology by treating humans as sensing animals, except he stresses the changes, introduced particularly by television, in the configuration of sensations confronting these animals. What the mode of information puts into question, however, is not simply the sensory apparatus but the very shape of subjectivity: its relation to the world of objects, its perspective on that world, its location in that world. We are confronted not so much by a change from a "hot" to a "cool" communications medium, or by a reshuffling of the sensoria, as McLuhan thought, but by a generalized destabilization of the subject. In the mode of information the subject is no longer located in a point in absolute time/space, enjoying a physical, fixed vantage point from which rationally to calculate its options. Instead it is multiplied by databases, dispersed by computer messaging and conferencing, decontextualized and reidentified by TV ads, dissolved and materialized continuously in the electronic transmission of symbols. In the perspective of Deleuze and Guattari, we are being changed from "arborial" beings, rooted in time and space, to "rhizomic" nomads who daily wander at will (whose will remains a question) across the globe, and even beyond it through communications satellites, without necessarily moving our bodies at all.[17]

The body then is no longer an effective limit of the subject's position. Or perhaps it would be better to say that communications facilities extend the nervous system throughout the Earth to the point that it enwraps the planet in a noosphere, to use Teilhard de Chardin's term, of language.[18] If I can speak directly or by electronic mail to a friend in Paris while sitting in California, if I can witness political and cultural events as they occur across the globe without leaving my home, if a database at a remote location contains my profile and informs government agencies which make decisions that affect my life without any knowledge on my part of these events, if I can shop in my home by using my TV or computer, then where am I and who am I? In these circumstances I cannot consider myself centered in my rational, autonomous subjectivity or bordered by a defined ego, but I am disrupted, subverted and dispersed across social space.

The study of the mode of information intersects to a certain extent with the study of mass or popular culture. TV ads and computerized shopping which are discussed below are also familiar topics to students of mass culture. In the 1980s the study of mass culture moved beyond the Frankfurt School's preoccupation with the manipulation of the masses by the culture industry, which is grounded in the privilege accorded to high culture as emancipatory. Stuart Hall and the program of "cultural studies" locate within popular groups points of resistance to dominant forms.[19] By contrast my study of the mode of information is more concerned with the manner and forms in which cultural experience constitutes subjects rather than with how groups of already constituted subjects resist or conform to the "external" demands of mass culture. This study connects more closely with the tendency in cultural studies to explore the way popular culture configures the masses as "feminine," as passive inferior, receptive.[20] As we shall see, the sectors of the mode of information also configure subjects as "other," as different from the cultural ideal of autonomous rationality. In the pages below I will be emphasizing the break with that ideal and exploring the possibilities, both liberatory and repressive, that it entails.

The broad purpose of this study is to explore the theoretical conditions for understanding the new configurations of the subject. Important limits of the study must be explicitly stated. The term "the mode of information" is not intended as a totalizing or essentializing category to control or inscribe a figure of the present age. It must be understood in the first instance as multiple: there are many modes of information each with its historical particularities and there are continuities and breaks between modes of information. In this study I do not attempt to generate a formal theory of the field of modes of information. I do not delineate concepts as Marx did with the mode of production and as Weber did with the theory of legitimate authority, in each case specifying and controlling areas of empirical investigation, or providing explanatory models to account for changes from one mode of information to another, or offering periodizing taxonomies. The reason for this theoretical modesty derives from cautions imposed by the theoretical strategies that seemed most appropriate and most suggestive to my study, theoretical strategies that are known as poststructuralist. This book then is a preliminary study that posits in a rudimentary fashion a mode of information in the current situation. It is an experiment that hopes to promote further theoretical development and empirical research.

A review of critical social theory led me to the conclusion that contemporary society ought not to be approached through action-centered models. This is so for two reasons. First, groups that hold the initiative in recent protest movements, such as women and minorities, have been inscribed by the metanarratives of liberalism and Marxism as "other." These grand theories appeal to the discontents of a rational subject (individual or collective) that is thought to be capable of emancipating itself from domination. Women and minorities are excluded from this process or at least are at the margins of the centered political drama. Thus when women and minorities took the spotlight of political opposition in the 1970s a certain dislocation was imposed upon earlier traditions of emancipatory theory, a dislocation which some feminist theories have addressed with particular force. In order to take into account the politics of the "other," critical social theory requires an epistemological overhaul in which the figure of the rational subject no longer serves as a ground or frame. We are thereby permitted to reconstruct the oppositions normal/deviant, majority/minority, masculine/feminine. In addition to feminist and subaltern theory, the poststructuralist positions of Foucault, Derrida, Lyotard, Deleuze and Baudrillard move precisely in this direction.[21] They provide an antidote to a false return to those emancipatory metanarratives that can no longer function as critical. They also caution us about and institute theoretical mechanisms against positioning the theorist, especially the male theorist, as a rational subject, as a central, privileged position in the movement of liberation.

The second cause for skepticism about action-centered theory is that the social scene appears to me increasingly composed of electronically mediated communications that expand upon and magnify the self-referential aspect of language. Instead of envisioning language as a tool of a rational, autonomous subject intent upon controlling a world of objects for the purpose of enhanced freedom, the new language structures refer back upon themevles, subverting referentiality and thereby acting upon the subject and constituting it in new and disorienting ways. Again the theoretical texts of the poststructuralists had already pioneered this forbidding, strange terrain. If poststructuralist positions appear doubly relevant to a reconstructed critical social theory, they also impose severe restrictions upon such a project. Oddly enough poststructuralists call into question theory itself if by theory one means a set of concepts that open a terrain for investigation by a strategy that produces discursive maps of the territory. My turn to poststructuralism thus precludes the development of a theory of the mode of information that displaces while mirroring the theory of the mode of production.

The strategy I adopt and the one enacted in this book follows a double imperative:[22] it locates sectors of electronically mediated communication and in each case invokes a poststructuralist position to highlight and examine the self-referential linguistic mechanism instantiated therein. The poststructuralist position illuminates the decentering effects of the electronically mediated communication on the subject and, reciprocally, the electronically mediated communication subverts the authority effects of the poststructuralist position by imposing the social context as a decentering ground for theory. Hence I couple TV ads and Baudrillard, databases and Foucault, electronic writing and Derrida, science and Lyotard. The intended result is to accomplish the intermediate task of drawing attention to some of the structurally new features of the contemporary social space and to promote interest in theories that brightly illuminate it. The topics I address are of course not the only possible ones: the telephone, photography, the cinema, to name only a few language wrappings not discussed below, are fully appropriate and even necessary topics within the thematic of the mode of information.

This book is not, of course the first to point in the general direction of a poststructuralist strategy for writing history. The work of Joan Scott in women's history, Lynn Hunt and Jean-Christophe Agnew in cultural history, Ernesto Laclau, Chant Mouffe, Dominick LaCapra and Alan Megill in social/historical theory, to mention only a few names, all anticipate the working through of poststructuralist theory in relation to questions of historical and social investigation. My effort is to focus on the point of intersection between new communication phenomena and poststructuralist theories, to explore the ramifications of that intersection as a step toward a more general discursive initiative that has variously been termed cultural studies, postmodern theory, subaltern discourse, local knowledges. I see these tendencies as part of a challenge to existing disciplines in the human sciences to ask new sorts of questions, ones that take as their point of departure a self-reflexive recontextualization, and that abandon "modern" positions in favor of exploring "postmodern" positions. I mean by this that the political metanarratives of emancipation from the eighteenth and nineteenth centuries that have served as frames and reference points for the disciplines of history, literature, philosophy, sociology, anthropology and so forth now appear to be losing their powers of coherence, their ability to provide a groundwork of assumptions that make it appear natural to ask certain questions and to think that the answers to those questions define the limit and extent of the problem of truth. I refer to questions such as the following: What is/was the condition of the working class at a certain time and place? How do/did political mechanisms ensure natural rights and overthrow arbitrary power? How does/did a given nation ensure its glory and power? How does/did an economy industrialize and secure continued growth? These questions along with many others like them have been some of the leading and animating issues of the human sciences. The time has come to question their hegemony over discourse, to propose new questions that the old ones subordinate, forget or repress, new questions that open political initiatives that may not easily fit into the cultural frame of liberal and socialist images of freedom and that may move to the "margins," to the new movements of the 1970s and 1980s. At this stage, however, it is too early in the development of the problematic to provide firm linkages between the forms of domination and potentials for freedom that the theory of the mode of information reveals, on the one hand, and the advances of feminism, minority discourse and ecological critiques, on the other. Only occasionally in the chapters that follow do I attempt to correlate my findings with discussions of gender, race and class.

I situate the theoretical and social origin of the mode of information within a field of contending discourses and imagine that it threatens the dominance of established positions. But I do not claim that the old questions are irrelevant or that they should be abandoned, only that they need to be relativized by new ones. To argue otherwise would amount to asserting not a contest of discourses but a pretense to exclusive reason, a claim that poststructuralist theory, to which I am indebted, denies from the outset. Yet I do assert the emergence of a certain "new," I do affirm a break with the modern, a discontinuity with current paradigms. And I do so knowing full well that this "new" electronically mediated communication or mode of information is in many ways not new at all, but has been anticipated in social developments and theoretical initatives for decades, even centuries. Electronically mediated information systems go back to the telegraph and photography of the nineteenth century.

But the problem is not to demonstrate the slow, continuous evolution of the past into the present, thereby creating a familiarity

1

The Concept of Postindustrial Society

Bell and the Problem of Rhetoric

> Is it not commonplace nowadays to say that the forces of man
> have already entered into a relation with the forces of information
> technology and their third-generation machines which together
> create something other than man, indivisible 'man-machine'
> systems? Is this a union with silicon instead of carbon?
>
> From Gilles Deleuze, *Foucault*

Recent efforts to generate a new theory of the contemporary social
world have met with great resistance. Notions of advanced capitalism,
for Marxists, and the idea of modernization, for Weberians, still
dominate their respective traditions of social theory and empirical
studies. In general, changes in the social order that have occurred in
the past few decades are explained within the old models. Alternative
rubrics – postindustrial society, information society, the third wave,
the atomic or nuclear or electronic age – have been considered and,
on the whole, rejected.

And yet things are happening in the social fabric, things that are
radically new and that are not well accounted for within the confines
of the established positions. It could be the case that students of
society are confronted with a paradigm shift, in the sense of Thomas
Kuhn, except that the anomalous instances, the elements that resist
the old frameworks, have not yet reached a critical mass or do not
yet constitute a large enough corpus to convince observers that
traditional positions need to be abandoned in favor of new ones. It
could equally be the case that recent social changes are comprehensible
within the existing frameworks.

Another possibility is that the issue is not the substitution of one
totalizing framework for another, but the elaboration of a regional

theory that accounts for the new phenomena. This is the position I would like to defend in the pages that follow. I want to affirm and to theorize the conditions for the study of a new historical sector, one that implies radical changes in the social order. Also as part of the theoretical conditions for the analysis of the new sector I want to argue against the notion of a totalizing theory. These are two distinct but related theoretical issues. I will argue that what is new in society is a set of structures of domination that are linguistically based, that one feature of these structures is their reliance on totalizing forms of discourse. Hence one problem for critical theory is to develop a form of discourse that does not repeat the totalizing quality of the discourses it proposes to analyze and unseat. The first deficiency therefore of concepts like "postindustrial society" is that they substitute one totalizing position for another.

Before presenting my critique of postindustrial theories I want to clarify my critique of totalizing theories. A distinction needs to be made between general theories and totalizing theories. A general theory specifies a field that encompasses the vast majority of society *at a specific level of analysis* or *for a defined portion of experience*. Demographics is an example of general theory. General theory becomes totalizing when it claims to include within its field all social phenomena, or the "essence" of society, in sum, when it marginalizes those perspectives or experiences that are not within its domain. As I use the term, totalizing theory disqualifies antagonistic perspectives and claims to exhaust the meaning of the entire social field, or less drastically, that portion of the social field that it theoretically constitutes as an object of study. Totalizing theories tend to dehistoricize the social field by grounding their positions in nature, the dialectic, reason, statistical calculations, and so forth. There is one moment of theory formation in which totalization cannot, indeed should not, be avoided. When the theorist selects his or her field or topic there is an implicit totalizing act since the selection is made from a field of all possible topics. In this sense alone, totalization is a condition for the possibility of any theory.

The Cunning of Totalization

The discursive effect of the term postindustrial society is to deny the validity of positions rooted in the analysis of industrial society. The theory of postindustrial society introduces a break in the strong sense, one that reduces to insignificance those social dimensions that precede the break. After the term postindustrial is introduced the social theorist can no longer claim as significant for analysis those features of society that belong to the industrial period. The theorist of postindustrialism has thus redefined social reality, has reconstituted the field of analysis, making invalid areas of experience that are not characteristic of the new model. This process of cancellation is the power effect of the totalizing term. Totalization introduces a theoretical zero–sum game, a game that has been played over and over again in the history of social theory, in which theories are pitted against one another like two bulls in springtime fighting for control of a group of cows. Regardless of the validity of the argument for the concept of postindustrialism, its totalizing character introduces a rhetorical gesture that elicits an equally totalizing response.

Daniel Bell, whose work is most closely associated with the theory of postindustrial society, commits the error of totalization in the strongest sense.[1] He defines postindustrial society in opposition to all previous social formations, encompassing the entire history of humanity in a schema that distinguishes the new from the old. Citing the statistical analysis of the US economy by Marc Porat, Bell concludes that "nearly fifty per cent of GNP, and more than fifty per cent of wages and salaries, derive from the production, processing and distribution of information goods and services. It is in that sense that we have become an information economy."[2] By contrast, in earlier societies income was largely derived from "extraction" or "fabrication." In addition to the distinction based on income sources, postindustrial society is unique, Bell contends, in that more than half the labor force now consists, for the first time in history, of information workers.[3] Bell's third criterion for postindustrial society derives from and develops further those of income and labor: knowledge and information are now the "axial principles" of society. In his words, "The axial principle of postindustrial society . . . [is] the centrality of theoretical knowledge . . ."[4] While he recognizes that all societies employ knowledge in production, he proposes that only recently has the economy become characterized by "a fusion of science and engineering . . ." For Bell the indices of income, labor and knowledge determine that a new social and economic structure has emerged, a postindustrial society.

Bell is far too astute a theorist to ignore completely the problem of totalization. He pretends to limit the definition of postindustrial society only to the level of economic and social structure, eschewing any attempt to characterize "the total configuration of society."[5] Yet on the very next page of his text one reads that postindustrial society is a change in "reality," one that gives priority to the social world and subordinates nature and things to it. The register has shifted from social analysis to ontology and the theorist's categories of analysis have become indexes of reality itself. In fact the issue is finally not that Bell does or does not limit his analysis to the social structure: throughout his work economic, political and cultural factors are swept up into a unified definition of postindustrial society.[6] The problem is rather that the rhetoric of totalization is integral to his problematic. The discursive act of defining the limits of new social phenomena is carried out by Bell in a register in which the definition of the new phenomena becomes the definition of the entire society.

Bell makes little effort to limit the scope of his analysis and therefore to avoid the impression that he is presenting a new totalization. The statistical analyses he uses are at the macrological level and his assertions about the character of postindustrial society are flat statements of general fact. For example, he presents a tripartite history of social "infrastructures" in which there is a progression from transportation systems, to energy systems, to mass communications systems. The change to postindustrial society occurs during the third stage when there occurs a merger of the mass media with the computer.[7] The social world is thus transformed by general processes that have no clear limits. What is most regrettable in all of this is that while Bell would eschew "technological determinism,"[8] he attributes the cause of postindustrial society to a *technical* innovation (the computer + mass media = postindustrial society), thus contradicting himself. Even if one grants Bell his slip into technological determinism the problem of totalization remains, for he depicts the entire field of social reality as uniformly and homogeneously affected by the introduction of computerized mass media.

Another difficulty in Bell's totalizing discourse is his use of social scientific language to validate and legitimize his theory of postindustrial society. Bell argues that with the coming of postindustrial society the major "variables" have changed from those of capital and labor to those of information and knowledge.[9] Bell here disguises the vagueness of his formulation by the use of the term "variable," which lends a precise, scientific aura to his statements. The statement asserts that knowledge is the independent variable in postindustrial society and that it determines other dependent variables, such as capital and labor. Formulated as a hypothesis, the statement might serve as a guide for future studies, but Bell presents it to the reader as a conclusion, transforming by the magic of rhetoric an assumption into a finding. The assertion assumes what in fact needs to be demonstrated by empirical studies.

Bell's proclamation that knowledge and information are now "the crucial variables" does more than violate the order of scientific method. The formulation is much too totalizing to be of much use in empirical social science. The terms are all wrong: capital, labor, knowledge and information are not comparable units of analysis. They cannot be "operationalized" in research like the categories of age, sex, race, income. Even if studies were done to demonstrate Bell's proposition they would not likely convince many observers because of the level of generality involved. We are back to the problem of totalization: one would need to have *all* the variables of society and carry out *all* possible correlations in order to conclude that the *chief* variables are knowledge and information. In short, Bell's claim that "knowledge and information are the crucial variables of postindustrial society" is a *theoretical* argument that is given the appearance of proven fact.

Bell may have used the term "variable" in a metaphoric sense in which the term means the important or leading phenomenon. In this case the difficulty in his position is precisely the question of the epistemological authority on which the judgment is based. The statement in question is performative[10] not constative. That knowledge and information are the leading variables of society is not known or proven but asserted by Bell. By dressing the assertion in the garb of science the author is doing things to the reader, commanding a reordering of the reader's perception of what is important in the social field. He is not merely transmitting knowledge. And this reordering is at the level of the social totality, not at the level of a particular phenomenon. It is no accident that Bell resorts to performative statements at the point in his argument where he is concerned with the totality. Since the totality cannot be *known* by situated individuals it must be *figured*,[11] usually in performative strategies like the one Bell uses.

The Repression of Language

If the conceptualization of postindustrial society is flawed by a rhetoric of totalization, it is also theoretically deficient when it represses the linguistic level of the phenomena that it designates as new. Theorists of postindustrialism tend to ignore the problem of language both at the level of theory and at the level of the constituted social field. Even though they give priority to phenomena like knowledge, information, and communication, they do not treat these phenomena as linguistic issues and they give no heed to the linguistic quality of their own discourse. This omission is serious and it mars the effort to present a coherent argument for postindustrial or information society. The problem speaks to the limit of a social science that refuses to concern itself with language theory, raising the important epistemological difficulty of the border between disciplines and their essential non-unity.[12]

Like Marx and Weber, Bell assumes that the social field consists of actions. As we have seen, he characterizes postindustrial society as a service economy with a majority of people working no longer in the extraction of raw materials or the fabrication of goods but in an information exchange or "game" between persons. Bell insists that the central feature of postindustrial society is the new role of knowledge and information in the economy. Indeed writers who argue in favor of a new social formation generally focus on information as the major theme of the emerging new economic world. They divine a new pattern of the production, distribution and consumption of information as the chief attribute of the new epoch. They all, Bell especially, treat information as a set of economic facts, thereby absorbing the new social phenomenon within the old categories of capitalist (or in some cases Marxist[13]) economic theory.

Bell is quick to notice the anomalous quality of information: unlike material goods, information is not exhausted in its consumption. The fact that one person gains information from a database does not reduce the ability of another to gain the same information. Everyone in fact may "have" the same information even at the same time. Scarcity of material resources, the prime axiom of capitalist economic theory, does not apply to information.[14] The edifice of capitalism appears to be threatened by the inexhaustibility of information, by its resistance to the commodity form. Instead of raising the theoretical question of the possibility of an economy beyond the limits of scarce commodities, Bell hurries to reconcile the new with the old. While information is not suited to spatial forms of scarcity it initiates a new form of scarcity, he contends, the scarcity of time. Information becomes a commodity to the extent that the time needed to reproduce it falls within the principles of capitalist economic theory. Bell and capitalist theorists generally have discovered that information, like automobiles, can be sold and therefore may fall within the market system. The price of information is determined for them by the same laws of supply and demand that govern the distribution of material commodities.

Bell thereby lends legitimacy to the extension of the commodity form to the new realm of information, reversing a longstanding liberal princple that, in a democracy, knowledge and information in general must be freely accessible. When Denis Diderot, the eighteenth-century liberal, included in his *Encyclopedia* detailed information about the production processes in the major crafts, he hoped to destroy the principle of secret knowledge that was a mainstay of the old guild system. The wealth of a democratic nation, he thought, depended upon the unimpeded circulation of scientific and technical information. It is something of a scandal that a major liberal thinker of the twentieth century, like Bell, should reverse this principle. Just when the merger of mass communications and the computer makes possible the rapid, universal distribution of information, and therefore in principle extends radically the democratization of knowledge, and thereby perhaps a deeper social democratization, Bell sees fit to authorize the restriction of information to those who can foot the bill. Capitalism thus extends the domain of crime to those who reproduce knowledge without authorization and those who access it without paying their fees. The exchange of information between individuals and groups, if Bell has his way, would fall within the commodity form, in the Marxian and Lukácsian sense, alienating and reifying yet another aspect of social relationships.

One feature of the electronic information works against its commodification. The new technologies advance considerably the reproducibility of information. The combination of electronic coding and recording on plastic tape surfaced with oxides enables the speedy and accurate copying of many forms of information: words, numbers, music, visual images. As the technologies that process and reproduce information are integrated with the technologies that move information through space (telecommunications systems) the prospects unfold for new patterns of communication, prospects that promise to introduce significant changes in the social order. The ease with which information can be reproduced or moved has already created havoc with a legal system that is articulated to protect the private ownership of material commodities. Copyright laws presume that copying is a difficult, expensive process, considerations that are made obsolete by the new electronic technologies. Laws governing the right to privacy presume that privacy is threatened by intrusions of people into the space of others, again no longer reflecting the state of the art of information gathering. And so it goes in one domain after another: the ability to disseminate information outstrips the protecting and restricting mechanisms of individual property.[15]

By treating information as an economic rather than as a linguistic fact the theory of postindustrial society obscures the question of the new communication possibilities of disseminating information opened up by the electronic technologies.[16] While it is certainly true that capitalism engulfs as much information as it can under the net of the laws of the market, the new structures of information, treated as linguistic phenomena, introduce changes in the pattern of communication in society and destabilize the positions of subjects in that society. One strategy that Bell uses to sidestep the issue of new communication patterns is to treat them only in a quantitative manner, thus extending his economic metaphor in a reductive manner while at the same time denying that the economic analysis is in any sense metaphoric. He recognizes that through the communications abilities of the mass media "the number of persons (and places) that one *knows of* accelerates at a steeply exponential rate."[17] The communications systems of postindustrial society thus increase in quantity the interactions between people.

To support the argument for the quantitative analysis of information, Bell cites theorists of cybernetics, like Shannon and Wiener, who treat communication as a physical and statistical relation between information and noise. Information is that part of a communication that is not "lost" in its transmission. The part that is lost, noise, is analogous to heat that is dissipated in the conversion of energy to matter. Cybernetic theorists resist somewhat the temptation completely to reduce information to a physicalist model. Some of them define information simply as the organization of matter and energy,[18] a definition that strictly speaking avoids reductionism but leaves unresolved the question of the status of information in relation to physics. In any case the model remains a quantitative one in which information holds a dubious, somewhat mystical relation to matter and energy.

In addition to quantifying linguistic phenomena, cybernetic theorists explicitly seek centralized control over communications. Norbert Wiener, for instance, includes within his definition of cybernetics both "the electrical engineering theory of the transmission of messages" and "the study of messages as a means of controlling machinery and society."[19] In principle, cybernetics is an elitist theory. It is a tool designed for technocrats better to manage what is seen as a chaotic society. Cybernetics is tainted by military orientation and sensibility, born as it was during the struggle with Hitler's

Germany. Wiener strategizes as follows: "the purpose of Cybernetics [is] to develop a language and techniques that will enable us indeed to *attack* the problem of control and communication in general."[20] Cybernetics is a theory for an armed camp preparing for a final struggle. But the politico-military atmosphere that pervades Wiener's text, which was written in the early 1950s when the US was in the grip of McCarthyite fever, is displaced from the contest with fascism and communism to the warfare with nature. Wiener again: "we are always *fighting* nature's tendency to degrade the organized and to destroy the meaningful . . ."[21] The "law" of entropy legitimates the just cause of the technocratic domination of language and the bureaucratic reduction of meaning to "electronic engineering."

On the basis of cybernetic theory Bell concludes that in postindustrial society information somehow increases and therefore communications are *better*. This more-is-better theory of communication effectively represses the major questions of the relation of language to society, restricting the theory of postindustrial society to an economic metaphor that is worthy only of the most simplistic versions of Marxism. For the question of a new stage in social theory begins just where Bell leaves off. If he is right to argue that some version of knowlege/information is a central "axis" of contemporary society, as I think he is, then the issue is not one of the economics of information but one of the qualitative transformation of social relations through the insertion into the historical field of new forms of communication. Bell effectively dissociates the question of the relation of communication and society by (1) reducing communication to an economic metaphor, and (2) shifting the issue of culture to a separate "axial principle" from that of society.[22]

The question that eludes the harbingers of postindustrial society is the nature of the transformations of language in the new social phenomena. Postindustrial theorists remain blind to recent transformations because they continue to use lenses designed to spot socio-economic targets. Certainly the new developments in the economy noted by Bell and others have occurred. But their claim that these changes constitute a fundamental reordering of society, the rise of a *post*industrial world, are vulnerable to the criticism, sounded by Marxists and others, that the changes are one of degree not one of kind. Service and information workers, like factory workers, such a position would maintain, remain salaried employees, subject to the capital–labor relation. Indeed much of the service and information sector of the economy is modeled closely on the factory. Fast food eateries produce assembly line hamburgers; many engineers are subject to a division of labor that rivals that of the assembly line workers depicted in the film *Modern Times*. While it is true that some jobs in the information sector encourage work democracy and creativity, these are limited to a small percent of the total.[23] Most information workers carry out tedious, repetitive tasks, earn low wages, have a low social status and work under regimented conditions. For them the prospect of postindustrial society harbingers only more of the dreary same.

Certainly there have been important changes in the economy in recent decades. Theorists of postindustrial society are right to point to such trends as the massive insertion of science in the economy, the changing composition of the workforce, the internationalization of production, and the fragility of complex, interdependent advanced technologies.[24] From the standpoint of critical social theory as I am using the term, these changes are less important in understanding the quality of social relations than are changes in the structure of communicative experience.

The Limits of Anticipation in Marx and Weber

A case can be made that Marx and Weber foresaw the social phenomena that I call the mode of information and accounted for them within the contours of their theories. At least, this position might maintain, one need not abandon completely the theories of Marx and Weber in order critically to comprehend the mode of information; one need only supplement their views to encompass new historical developments. While this position has some merit,[25] I argue that the action-based theories of Marx and Weber have only limited ability to grasp the linguistic mechanisms that are at the heart of the mode of information. The considerable ability of the discourses of Marx and Weber to anticipate the direction of things to come speaks to the extraordinary vision embedded in their theories. Yet even these prescient thinkers were not able completely to overcome their historical circumstances. Their mental worlds were limited by certain cultural assumptions that precluded an adequate conceptualization of structures of communication. At least this is what I will try to demonstrate below.

By the late 1850s, at the time he wrote the *Grundrisse*, Marx discerned with great clarity that the process of automation – the substitution of machines for human labor and the accompanying change in the organic composition of capital – was undermining the most basic principle of political economy: the labor theory of value. Since Marx was a *critic* of the theory of political economy, his position relied on the labor theory of value only to the extent that he needed it to demonstrate the *internal* contradiction of capitalism. To Marx, the labor contract was not an equal exchange but a process of exploitation in which workers did not receive all that they gave. Marx was able fully to face the prospect that capitalism could develop the process of production to the point that labor woud become only an adjunct to it. He stated explicitly that "to the degree that large industry develops, the creation of real wealth comes to depend less on labour time and on the amount of labour employed than on the power of the agencies set in motion during labour time . . ."[26] This process of the substitution of machine for human will advance to the point, Marx predicted, that production will proceed virtually without the participation of workers. Marx continues his analysis: "Labour no longer appears so much to be included within the production process; rather, the human being comes to relate more as watchman and regulator to the production process itself. . . . [The worker then] steps to the side of the production process instead of being its chief actor."[27]

Needless to say, in these circumstances, the capitalist mode of production has been turned inside out. Machines "work"; human beings supervise. Under such unprecedented conditions, the prospects of proletarian revolt and the hopes for socialist transformation would appear to be considerably changed, outcomes that were certainly of great interest to Marx and could not have escaped his attention. Yet he writes not a word about it. Instead he simply states that these conditions signify the emergence of the "social individual," in other words, socialism itself. Marx's text on this point is worth quoting at length:

> In this transformation, it is neither the direct human labour he himself performs, nor the time during which he works, but rather the appropriation of his own general productive power, his understanding of nature and his mastery over it by virtue of his presence as a social body – it is, in a word, the development of the social individual which appears as the great foundation-stone of production and of wealth. The *theft of alien labour time, on which the present wealth is based*, appears a miserable foundation in face of this new one, created by large-scale industry itself. As soon as labour in the direct form has ceased to be the great well-spring of wealth, labour time ceases and

must cease to be its measure, and hence exchange value . . . of use value.[28]

In this extraordinary passage Marx foresees the ultimate consequences of automation: the disappearance of exploitation and alienation. The creation of socialism, the appearance of "the social individual," is a result of the *internal* development of capitalism. In this passage at least Marx is a technological determinist.

Of greater interest to us in this passage, however, is Marx's recognition of the role of science in the process of automation. Again his acumen is remarkable: automation depends "on the general state of science and on the progress of technology, or the application of this science to production."[29] In another formulation he writes, "The development of fixed capital indicates to what degree general social knowledge has become a *direct force of production*."[30] The substitution of science for labor as the chief force of production is *inevitable*: capital, Marx asserts, "calls to life all the powers of science and of nature . . . in order to make the creation of wealth independent (relatively) of the labour time employed on it."[31] As the future unfolds for the historical materialist, the critique of political economy resembles the genre of science ficton. The capitalist becomes some sort of alien whose superior powers invoke at will the forces of knowledge and matter.

Like his analysis of the changing role of the worker in the labor process, Marx's discussion of the new status of science as a force of production is strangely inadequate. Above all else Marx was a thinker who was most sensitive to the social implications of changes in the mode of production. Yet here he seems only concerned with drawing attention to the internal contradictions of capital. He points unmistakably to tremendous transformations of the production process on the horizon, but fails to note even briefly the likely impact of these changes on his theory of the mode of production. For example, if science is a force of production, does the distinction between the base and superstructure collapse? Or is it necessary to include scientists in the category of labor? If so, what becomes of the description of the workers as an impoverished class with "nothing to lose but its chains"? And what becomes of the split between mental and manual work as a chief component of the division of labor under capitalism? Since Marx has determined that automation is an imminent inevitably, not a remote possibility, it would appear that these questions carry a degree of urgency that belies his silence about them. Indeed the whole intellectual apparatus of historical materialism, as well as that of the theory of political economy, is put in doubt by the changes Marx outlines.

Science, as Marx states, is a form of knowledge, a discourse. As such it cannot be examined, from the perspective of critical social theory, by use of the concepts designed to reveal the structures of the domination of labor. The production, distribution and consumption of science, to employ economic categories, are governed by a different logic from those of labor. The theoretical step from a notion of the emancipation of the labor act to liberation of scientific discourse is not obvious and requires drastic conceptual reformulation. When the transformation of natural materials into commodities is mediated not simply by manual labor operating on machines but by scientific discourses, discourses that are tied to research institutions, government granting agencies, the apparatuses of journals, and the social ritual of conferences, then the master/slave relation of capital and labor has become unrecognizably changed.

The profound mediation of the production process by scientific discourse calls into question many of the underlying assumptions of Marx's cultural world. Marx could reasonably argue, as in the *Theses on Feuerbach*, for a transformed materialism that would incorporate idealism as the active side of practice. He wanted to assure due recognition to conscious intelligence as part of human bodies moving in space and time. But he was most concerned with a theory that would account for the new ways in which bodies were moving in space and time, in short, the organization of labor activity. His theory was shaped by the assumptions of a nineteenth-century culture still profoundly indebted to the Enlightenment, with its oppositions of man/nature, subject/object, mind/body, idealism/materialism, reason/unreason. In the context of these oppositions, the place of science was fixed on the side of man, subject, mind, idealism, reason. Science was an act of human intelligence, dispelling the mists of religion, defining the processes of nature. It was at once a tribute to human beneficence, a tool for "the relief of man's estate," and a progressive force in the struggle for freedom. The commitment of Marx to science is displayed, for example, in his appreciation of the work of Darwin.

The entwinement of science and industry, to paraphrase Horkheimer and Adorno,[32] necessitates a strategy of analysis that is free of these Enlightenment assumptions. Science must be analyzed as a set of discourses and practices that both works to eliminate toil *and* extend the powers of dominant social forces. After science becomes a legitimate form of discourse and is integrated into established institutions (the corporation, the state, the schools, even the military) it is dangerous. Cognitive activities associated with science cannot be distinguished by critical social theory as purely mental phenomena, but must be examined as political forces, a shift in perspective that Marx did not achieve.

The neoMarxists of the Frankfurt School did attempt such a reorientation. Horkheimer and Adorno in *Dialectic of Enlightenment*, Marcuse in *One-Dimensional Man* and Habermas in "Science and Technology as Ideology," each in different ways adjusted the concept of science to account for its new role in advanced industrial society. They worked with the opposition science/ideology, underscoring the role of science in legitimating the dominant forces in the capitalist mode of production. For them science had an *original* meaning that was associated with reason and emancipation,[33] with dispelling ideology in the forms of religion, myth, superstition.

In *Dialectic of Enlightenment*, Horkheimer and Adorno argue that science, although it had this progressive function, is also associated with domination, the domination of nature. The objectifying aspect in the epistemology of science is the basis for the domination of nature as other. This "flaw" in science would prove its undoing as a progressive force. When scientific epistemology is adopted in the social/cultural field, as in modern advertising or what Horkheimer and Adorno term "the culture industry," human beings become the subject of domination and science becomes ideology. The formulation of the problem of science by Horkheimer and Adorno is restricted to the level of epistemology. It descends to the arena of everyday life in such essays by Adorno as "The Stars Down to Earth,"[34] and "On the Fetish Character in Music and the Regression in Listening,"[35] effectively demonstrating the conservative function of popular culture. The limit of this analysis, however, rests with the understanding of discourse as superstructural content, not as form. The astrology column in the *Los Angeles Times* and the pop music radio broadcast are understood by Adorno as semantic conditioning effects. What is ignored are the structural effects of the discourses, the mechanisms by which are established the conditions for the "conditioning effects." In his fascinating essay, "How to Look at Television," Adorno sociologically analyzes the audience and psychoanalytically analyzes the stereotyped content of serialized programs, but treats the communicational structure of television only in passing.[36] In short, Adorno did not theorize the communicational structure of the newspaper, radio and television as lingustic phenomena, or examine the way they are able to constitute the receiver of the message in such a manner that he or she is subject to the influence of the media.

A similar problem detracts from the critique of science as ideology by Marcuse and Habermas. In *One-Dimensional Man* Marcuse limits the critique to the epistemological level. To take one example from empirical sociology, the Hawthorne study by Mayo is ideological, according to Marcuse, because of its positivist assumptions (a critique, it might be mentioned, that could also be leveled at Adorno's *The Authoritarian Personality*). Because positivism operationalizes the social field, Marcuse contends, it politicizes class antagonisms and in general dehistoricizes its object. While Marcuse's argument is powerful and, in my view, has never been refuted by empirical sociologists,[37] it also fails to capture the structural effects of social science discourse. In the second half of the twentieth century, the widespread application of social science to major institutions (the corporation, welfare agencies, primary education, penal institutions and so forth), shapes the social world through the power effects of discourse. The problem is not that social science is ideological when it undermines working class critiques of capitalism in the factory, but that it *institutes* practices that bear domination within them.[38] Like Horkheimer and Adorno, Marcuse's critique of science assumes a dualist world of subjects and objects in which science objectifies subjects and thus becomes ideological.

Habermas developed his position on the question of science in an essay of 1968 entitled "Technology and Science as 'Ideology'."[39] Responding directly to Marcuse's *One Dimensional-Man*, Habermas complained that Marcuse had not adequately specified the way science becomes politically conservative in advanced capitalist society.[40] In order to correct this deficiency, Habermas turned to Max Weber's theory of science as instrumental action (*Zweckrationalität*). Before pursuing Habermas's analysis of Weber, I will turn to consider Weber's position in its own right since it has been a general subject of interest to social theorists and bears great importance for the question of postindustrial society. (As a reminder to the reader, let me restate the question at hand: to what extent did Weber anticipate the phenomena I am designating with the term mode of information? And therefore to what extent can classical social theory account for the mode of information.)

Weber's theory of social action lends itself, more readily than Marx's, to an understanding of communicational and linguistic experience. For Weber, unlike Marx, grounded his account of the transformation of society toward modernity in a theory of action that did not privilege labor but distinguished types of action in terms of their meaning for the individual insofar as they take other people into account.[41] To this extent Weber's is a subjective theory of social interactions. He then distinguished four types of such action: instrumental rational, value rational, affectual and traditional. The interest and passion of Weber's work lies in his analysis of how modernity, defined as the spread of instrumental action, comes to reverse the relation of reason and domination. With great acumen Weber understood that modern society institutionalized instrumental reason in the form of bureaucracy. Once established, bureaucracy transformed instrumental reason into domination, a reversal that could not be accounted for within the paradigm of liberal (and Marxist?) thought.

The paradox and the pathos of modern society (both capitalist and socialist) is that it presumes individual freedom, defined as the capacity of rational choice, thereby rejecting all forms of domination characteristic of earlier social systems.[42] At the same time, modern society institutes a form of organization (bureaucracy) which constitutes a new type of domination. Weber thus conceptualizes the inconceivable: a social system that is at once rational and irrational in its core. It is rational because bureaucratic organization presumes that individuals act instrumentally. They cannot operate otherwise. Individuals fill out the appropriate forms because it is in their rationally determined interest to do so; if no one fills out the forms bureaucracy collapses. And yet, bureaucracy becomes a form of domination, an "iron cage" in Weber's words, that presents, in his view, the most formidable obstacle to change that has ever been institutionalized. The reason for the rigidity of bureaucracy – and herein lies the nub of Weber's thought – is that it is not open to rational critique. Since bureaucracy is already defined as a rational form of institution it cannot be attacked by theories which presume the legitimacy of instrumentally rational action. And final step in the logic: since theory itself, as opposed to religion or myth, presumes rationality as the basis of action, and since critique and revolution can only proceed on the basis of theory, bureaucracy is *invulnerable to known forms of theoretical critique and social change.*[43]

One difficulty with Weber's position concerns the place of science in bureaucratic society. Science, of course, has become bureaucratized, a problem that we may leave aside for now. More germane to this study is the problem that science, as a form of reason, is not seen by Weber as a political problem. After all, one of Weber's great accomplishments is to have shown that, in modern society, reason becomes domination. But, curiously enough, Weber is silent on the fate of science in modern society. Does it not also become a form of domination? In Weber's discourse, science is uniquely and peculiarly privileged. It enjoys a neutral space beyond politics and ideology. In "'Objectivity' in Social Science and Social Policy," Weber argues that, while values or politics animate the work of the social scientist, leading him or her to select a particular problem for investigation, the *validity* of scientific categories (ideal types) derives from their universal acceptance as guides to research, not from their political or normative character.[44] In "Science as a Vocation," Weber again makes a sharp distinction between science and politics.[45] Yet science is crucial to the development of modern society, not only with respect to the role of natural science in industry, but especially with respect to the role of social science in society.

Weber's position was clear: bureaucracy is dependent on science. He writes, "Bureaucratic administration means fundamentally domination through knowledge. This is the feature of it which makes it specifically rational."[46] The bureaucratic control and management of modern society requires up-to-date information about the population, information which the bureaucracy gathers itself but which also is provided by social scientists. Weber's work, along with that of the rest of his colleagues in sociology, *directly* contributes to bureaucratic domination. Weber offers no attempt to distinguish between the epistemology of bureaucratic knowledge and that of sociological knowledge. Since the "truth" of the discourses of bureaucracy and sociology are identical, Weber's writings contribute to the very process of domination in modernity that he deplores.

One can only conclude that something is lacking in Weber's theory, something that would permit one to distinguish between the rationality of sociology (or critical theory) and the rationality of bureaucracy. I suggest that what is lacking in Weber is a theory of communicative action that is linguistically based, such as the theory I am developing here as the mode of information.[47] Weber's discourse cannot account for recent developments in modern society because his position, like Marx's, is rooted in a theory of action, a dualism of action and consciousness, that has difficulty grasping linguistic mechanisms. Theories that are able critically to account for linguistic phenomena effectively bypass the dilemma of science vs. ideology, as I hope to demonstrate below.

In addition to the epistemological problem in Weber's writing, his sociology has difficulty in accounting for the mode of information insofar as it concerns social forms of language. As a theory of social *action*, Weberian social science is not set up to decipher a society that increasingly is characterized by electronically mediated forms of information exchange. In fact the central phenomenon illuminated by Weber's theory, bureaucracy, is best viewed as a crude form of a data storage and retrieval system, in short, a computer. As Weber understood them, bureaucracies are not political; they merely carry out policies by applying rules to individual cases *in relation to the knowledge they have of the cases.* The core of bureaucracy is knowledge or information. They are able to act, Weber writes, only on the basis of "a store of documentary material" that is available to them.[48] The files of a bureaucracy are identical in principle to a computer database and it is the database that governs the action of the bureaucrat. The database, not the bureaucrat, determines how each individual is treated. In this sense Weberian theory illuminates a democratic side of the database function of computers.

The political problem of bureaucratic domination derives not only from the power inherent in the social action of bureaucratic organization, but from the monitoring and surveillance functions accomplished by computerized databases. The Weberian theory of bureaucracy needs to be recast therefore into the problem of the linguistic forms in computerized databases. In sum, the power of bureaucracy derives in good part from the linguistic form instituted by computerized databases, the code which generates a form of language without ambiguity. Once this form of language is instituted it can be electronically transmuted for rapid transport through space and instant retrieval. Without these characteristics that are inherent in computerized databases bureaucracy would become ineffectual in monitoring and controlling modern populations, with their enormous numbers. Without computers it would not be possible to run the social security system, the welfare system, the mails and so forth. Put differently, it would require the labor of the entire workforce to administer that workforce. In this regard one point must be kept in mind: the establishment of modern surveillance and control is not simply a result of a technical innovation, that is, the computer. It requires the encoding of language (ASCII) so that symbols can be converted into electronic forms. A full analysis of the discursive power effects of databases appears below in chapter 3.

Thus Weber moved social theory in the direction of the mode of information, but he was unable to carry forward his position because (1) he remained locked in a theory of action/consciousness, (2) he privileged scientific discourse, and (3) his theory was couched in the Enlightenment problematic of reason/domination. Jürgen Habermas attempted to transcend the limits of Weber's position with a concept of symbolic interaction and, later, communicative interaction.

Habermas agrees with Weber that Marx's theory of the mode of production is an inadequate basis for comprehending modern society. Modernity witnesses "an expansion of subsystems of purposive-rational [instrumental] action and thereby calls into question the traditional form of the legitimation of power."[49] Habermas understands Weber as arguing that capitalism sets the basis for the extension of instrumental action to "all areas of life: the army, the school system, health services, and even the family [in addition to the market and the bureaucratic state]."[50] For the individual, these institutions are legitimated and appear to be rational since they eschew traditional forms of domination. The Marxist critique of modernity is limited to posing the alternative of socialism as a more rational form of non-traditional legitimacy. But beginning in the late nineteenth century, Habermas asserts, the rise of the interventionist state and the entry of science into industry limit the cogency of the socialist position.

The first issue is political. The problem of system maintenance shifts from the labor–capital relation to the state's need to legitimate its entry into the economy. Economic actions on the part of the state reveal the political aspect of capitalist relations. They no longer appear as a convergence of natural laws and individual instrumental actions; they are no longer "neutral" mechanisms that serve self-interest, but are subject to "manipulation" by "outside" parties. When the state intervenes in the market – welfare, military purchases, legal restrictions, arbitrating labor disputes – the economy loses its appearance of self-regulation. The secrets of capitalism are laid bare; what had been legitimate now reveals itself as ideological.[51] The contradiction of the social system has shifted from the Marxist to the Weberian problematic.

The second issue, the entry of science into the economy, is more directly our concern. For Habermas, if the interventionist state works to *politicize* the economy, the development of science serves to *depoliticize* it. Weber's theory of rationality failed to account for this impact of science on society. Marcuse's critique of science as ideology failed, Habermas contends, to move beyond the Marxist framework. Big science, as it has been called, makes state intervention legitimate by reintroducing "neutrality" to political action. When the government acts "technically," on a "scientific" basis, to solve a problem its action is automatically legitimate. The government employs the scientific "experts" to gain knowledge that is not available to the citizenry. The people then must approve state action. At least that is the tendency of politics in late capitalism. The same rule applies to corporations who employ scientists for research to generate new products that both simulate and make "scientific" the economy.

But these new roles for science call into question the legitimacy of instrumental rational action. Science is no longer a pure application of cognitive mental functions to the knowledge and control of nature for "the relief of man's estate" (Francis Bacon). Since science in advanced capitalism is crucial to the functioning of the economy and the strength of the state, one can no longer argue that it is "neutral," as Weber did. In addition the loss of neutrality by science brings into question the nature and limits of instrumental rational action. If the truth function of science can no longer be separated from politics/economics, instrumental reason itself can no longer be the basis of legitimate action in modern society. This is the crux of Habermas's analysis of science in contemporary society.

To overcome the limits of the theory of modernity in Marx, Weber and Marcuse, Habermas offers a new critical category: symbolic interaction, or in his later writing, communicative action. In the late twentieth century mankind is at a great crossroads. Until now the project of emancipation (or human progress) was based on the extension of (instrumental) reason to society. The human race advanced when it gained knowledge of its situation and applied that knowledge to life. The issue now is that this form of adaptive action itself has become non-adaptive, retrogressive, or a form of domination.[52] Future progress, Habermas argues, depends on *"removing restrictions on communication,"* a new form of legitimate action that he terms "the ideal speech situation."[53] He has thus shifted the ground of critical social theory from instrumental rational action to symbolic rational interaction. The conditions for the exchange of symbols between individuals, not their actions, is now the subject of theory. Habermas had moved from a theory of action to a theory of language. He has thus in part anticipated the concept of the mode of information.

Habermas's linguistic turn, however, fails to provide a framework for the analysis of electronically mediated communication for two reasons. First, he focuses in the first instance on a different issue, on the ground for emancipation, not the analysis of domination. At issue here is a judgment about what is needed to further a critical theory of contemporary society.

Habermas's focus on the ideal speech situation reflects his concern with the collapse of traditional grounds for emancipatory movements (the integration of the Western working class into society, the development of "actually existing socialism" as new forms of authoritarianism, and the inversion of instrumental reason into domination, the emergence of feminism and other "new social movements" to displace traditional working-class politics). The second reason is more serious and, unlike the first, not a matter of a choice of theoretical strategy.

Habermas's concept of communicative action attempts to preserve an Enlightenment notion of reason. The conditions of the ideal speech situation are that individuals seek consensus by adhering to "the universal validity claims" of "truth, rightness and truthfulness" in symmetrical or equal relationships.[54] The sum of these conditions is now the definition of reason to Habermas. The problem with this formulation is not so much that such conditions are impossible. Rather it is that they constitute an historico-ontological ground, one that has been defined by the theorist. In this case, the relation between the theorist and the population that is to adopt the theory remains instrumental: the theorist is the subject, the population is the object; the theorist reasons, the population acts. The Cartesian and capitalist division between the mental and the manual, theory and practice, mind and matter has been preserved in Habermas's argument, a relic of the past that contradicts his own notion of communicative action. Reason has once again become a form of domination, this time of the critical theorist over the movement of emancipation.

Invoking the traditional category of reason, Habermas also resorts to a strategy of totalization. For the veracity of the concept of the ideal speech situation cannot be demonstrated by logic alone. By a reading of Austin, Habermas is aware that speech acts are more than constative truth claims. The notion of the ideal speech situation is in part illocutionary, an act that does something to the reader. So it is not enough for Habermas to describe his concept to his readers and expect them to accept the implications of the argument and act accordingly. Since communications involve an element of rhetorical force and since Habermas has excluded rhetorical force from his own "ideal speech situation," his own authorial presence, he must legitimate his argument on grounds that do not derive from within its elements. For that purpose Habermas resorts to a totalizing historical gesture. He asserts that the ability of individuals in advanced industrial society to adhere to the ideal speech situation (in short, their communicative competence) is the pinnacle of the historical development of mankind.[55]

Habermas's judgment about the totality of human evolution leads him to defend his theory on universal grounds.[56] The theory of the ideal speech situation is valid for everyone because communicative competence is normatively the highest stage of human development. Like Hegel and Marx, Habermas contextualizes his argument not to define the contingent limits of his position but to universalize or absolutize it. The illocutionary result of this strategy is to render the theorist invulnerable to the objections of the reader. Hegel's Absolute Spirit, Marx's Proletariat and Habermas's ideal speech situation are similar speech acts in that they totalize history in order to legitimate theory as universal. To that extent they all work against the project of emancipation they seek to promote. In sum, Habermas has lifted the veil of repression that relegated language to the superstructure in critical social theory. But he reintroduced an element of totalization into his theory thereby preventing the development of an adequate basis for a critique of the mode of information.

In conclusion, serious deficiencies in the positions of postindustrial theorists, Marxists and Weberians prevent them from advancing a theory of the mode of information. In particular, the tendency to totalize, the inability to develop a linguistically based theory of information and the penchant for privileging the epistemological status of science all contribute to this impasse. In the chapters that follow I will attempt to show how certain "poststructuralist" theories assist in the reconstruction of critical social theory.

modernization thesis – is at work in Luhmann's position on the media. The motive for this incoherent mixture of Keatsian values with money and power (why not add fame?) is the immense theoretical problem of social unity. Media are the sinews, for Luhmann and Parsons, that hold together the differentiated institutions of modern society.

A more appropriate definition might be systems of communication that structure an unknown group of receivers, that have, in other words, an abstract audience. In this case the media are centers of information, distributing discourses and images to a broad public. In that respect they play a role not dissimilar to Foucault's "universal intellectual," a role that is the opposite of Gramsci's organic and traditional intellectuals. The media, in this definition, are systems of cultural transmission without ties to any community, either rural or urban; they are emitters of signals received by a tele-anomic society. In *No Sense of Place*, Meyrowitz contends that the media's peculiar relation to its audience drastically rearranges the social order. Basing his position on Erving Goffman's work,[2] Meyrowitz argues that the media change society by mixing audiences normally kept separate in the course of daily life. Electronic media blur the lines between institutionally structured subgroups. Backstage behavior in Goffman's sense, intimate talk shared only among close peers, informal conversations that solidify ties between people of a distinct outlook become accessible, through television and other media, to everyone.

For Meyrowitz the technical achievement of television is to nullify the effects of time and space distances, making possible asynchronous "gatherings" of heterogeneous populations.[3] He contends that the preservation of a social order based on hierarchic difference requires that each person in each status level have a "sense of place." The print media and literacy generally, according to him, never threatened this conservative principle since they preserved the separation of socially distinct groups. He attributes the success of the women's movement to these "shifts in communication technology."[4] While such claims have limited validity at best, Meyrowitz's basic position is suggestive: "media are types of social settings that include and exclude, unite or divide people in particular ways."[5] His thesis might help to explain the spread of cosmopolitan attitudes, the relative diminution of the narrow parochialism so common in earlier centuries. But it overlooks the role of politics in the process of change: sitcoms depicting ethnic, racial and low status groups – blacks, gays, single-parent families – only replaced shows like *Father Knows Best* after the radical movements of the 1960s effectively challenged the "middle-class" values that earlier seemed so stable. The hypothesis that TV followed and perhaps reinforced political change is just as plausible as Meyrowitz's alternative view.

An adequate account of the force of the media must move beyond the behavioral aspects of conversations, the dramaturgical model, to confront the problem of communications practice at the level of language. As their proponents claim, the electronic media do alter the time–space parameters of social interactions, in principle rendering anyone capable of communicating with anyone else at any time. Visions of McLuhan's global village are *in principle* a technical possibility. But such communications at a distance are *in practice* new structures of discourse. Older models of communicative interactions based on face-to-face or print situations are not simply expanded or multiplied by their electronic mediation. The mediation changes the structure, the conditions that underlie symbolic exchange. It may be the case that anyone may now talk with anyone else at any time but the words will no longer mean exactly the same things.

For one thing, electronically mediated conversation cancels *contexts*, creating new speech situations. The television set is a new speech context, one radically different from the past in that the speaker (understood as the entire apparatus of the broadcast) controls the context to a hitherto unimaginable extent. From the trivial (the background surface coloring of newscasters coordinated with their clothing)[6] to the serious (the camera angle of Lt Col. North during the Iran–Contra hearings makes him appear heroic even in a setting where the interrogators are positioned above the witnesses to reduce the force of the latters' statements), electronic media make scenarios of conversations by controlling contexts. To the extent that language is always contextual, that part of the meaning of words derives from where they are uttered, the mode of information introduces a new language that occurs in places unrelated to the material limitations of everyday life. Hence words and gestures emitted by broadcasters and received by individuals are tele-language, a new form of English.

Second, the media conversation is primarily *monologic*, not dialogic. One communications pole transmits virtually all of the messages; the other simply receives. For three, four or five hours a day, individuals tune in, voluntarily becoming spectator-participants, mutely receiving messages, choosing to observe, but observing selectively. The spectator recipient is structured to constitute his or her own programming schedule from the available offerings. But that is the extent of active involvement. At first glance the selection by television viewers of the mute position of receiver is perplexing:

why is it that people generally prefer the monologue of the tube over interactive conversation and print? Can it be that a show like *Santa Barbara* is more interesting than one's relatives, friends and the infinite corpus of the printed word? Perhaps conversation is anxiety inducing, as psychologists claim, and reading is mental aerobics. The answer I propose is that in receiving the monologic talk of the media one is not simply passive. The media promote forms of self-constitution by viewers that profoundly engage them. I will address this issue at length in the pages that follow.

Third, the monologic contextless media language is *self-referential*. While all language is to some degree self-referential, media language is so to a greater degree than most in proportion to its distance from context and its monologic character. The more a language/practice is removed from the face-to-face context of daily life in a stable culture in which social relationships are reproduced through dialogue, the more language must generate and reproduce those features from within itself; in other words, the media must simulate its context and ventriloquize its audience. The language/practice of TV absorbs the functions of culture to a greater degree than face-to-face conversations or print and its discursive effect is to constitute subjects differently from speech or print. Speech constitutes subjects as members of a community by solidifying the ties between individuals. Print constitutes subjects as rational, autonomous egos, as stable interpreters of culture who, in isolation, make logical connections from linear symbols. Media language replaces the community of speakers and undermines the referentiality of discourse necessary for the rational ego. Media language – contextless, monologic, self-referential – invites the recipient to play with the process of self-constitution, continuously to remake the self in "conversation" with differing modes of discourse. Since no one who knows the recipient is speaking to them and since there is no clearly determinate referential world outside the broadcast to provide a standard against which to evaluate the flow of meanings, the subject has no defined identity as a pole of a conversation.

These features of media language apply differentially to each type of media and, regarding television, to each type of broadcast. The TV ad most exemplifies the new features of media language and is therefore most appropriate as a subject for the analysis of the mode of information.

The TV Ad as Social Event

The TV ad is a widely experienced social event, one unique to the mode of information. The TV ad is a performative semiotic phenomenon: it employs words and images in order to effect changes in the behavior of the recipient of the message. Its aesthetic effects are not sublime; the information it transmits has little truth value; the moral attitudes it conveys are not exemplary; the desires it arouses elude the dynamics of the libido. The TV ad does not conform to any of Habermas's universal pragmatics of communication; it satisfies no validity claims – it does not count as true to the participants and represents nothing in the world; it expresses nothing intended by speakers; and it fulfills no socially redeeming value. TV ads are things one leaves room for, fastforwards past, curses at with impatience. They are truly degraded phenomena, universally scorned, resented, mocked and at best tolerated. And yet, I contend, they are crucial semiotic indices to an emerging new culture.

What happens when an individual watches a TV ad? We know that the average person watches thousands of them a year, perhaps hundreds of thousands of them in a lifetime. Television viewing is a major social activity in advanced industrial society; in time spent it is second only to work and sleep. TV ads are watched by all social groups, though the very young, the very old and housewives are apparently the most devoted audiences. Time spent in front of the tube is time taken away from other activities: from conversing with family and friends, from religious rites, from political organizing, from career building, from leisure activities, from community life. It is difficult to deny that people prefer to watch television to all these activities and that television viewing is the single most sought-after voluntary activity in contemporary American society. Free time is most synonymous with TV time. This is so in spite of the low regard which the tube suffers in many quarters.[7] When an individual watches a TV ad the chief social relation of society is reproduced.

What happens when an individual watches a TV ad? A great deal of effort goes into producing the ad. High salaries are paid in ad agencies and production costs are considerable. Pressure on agencies is intense to have successful ads and pressure on television stations is more intense to carry the message to as many people as possible. If cost is the criterion, ads must be regarded as among the most important elements of the economy. Ads are also in a central structural position in the economy, overlapping both the means and relations of consumption. The major problem of the capitalist economy since the 1920s shifted from production to consumption. Mankind's age old battle with nature for scarce resources began to change from the question of efficient production to the challenge of maximum consumption. In the second half of the twentieth century this challenge has been fought in the diminutive arena of the 30-second ad on the 19-inch TV. When an individual watches a TV ad the health of the economy is at stake.

Recently there have been threats to the supremacy of the TV ad. Video tape recorders permit viewers to skim past ads or to watch movies without ads. Like so many other new technologies (the photocopy machine, the audio tape recorder, etc.) the VCR provides the ability to reproduce information cheaply, quickly and easily. It puts the viewer in control of the images he or she views. Some cable channels provide freedom from ads in exchange for monthly fees. Both the VCR and pay TV are means to bypass the TV ad. But it is not clear that such an evasion is desirable. So successful is the practice of the TV ad that it has expanded its domain from commodities to public service messages, political campaign tactics, military recruitment, and religious donations. In what must be its final apotheosis, the TV ad is now the sole subject of one cable channel which combines advertising, retailing and distribution on a nonstop basis. The complete circulation of commodities is concentrated in the single act of TV watching. In response to the offer presented on TV, the viewer phones in his or her order, witnessing his or her own act of consumption as it occurs. When an individual watches this TV ad, he or she is on TV, both subject and object of the communication.

Causes and Effects

It is difficult to escape the conclusion that TV ads are major social events, prominent features of the social landscape of advanced industrial society. They are a recurrent, widespread phenomenon which are perceived as highly significant by corporate executives, politicians, religious figures and social critics. Beyond the recognition of their general importance looms the problem of how to interpret the ads. The strategy most often taken is to regard the ads as causes or independent variables, economic or sociocultural, and to attempt to measure their effects as the dependent variables of individual behavior, whether it be purchasing a commodity or stealing an object. One of the frustrations of social science and of market research in particular has been the inability to establish clear correlations between TV ads and consumer behavior. For the market researcher it is enough to indicate that sales of a product rose after an ad was run, assuming no other pertinent variables intervened. But the self-interest of capitalists provides a poor standpoint from which to glean social knowledge.

The standpoint of market research is limited by the instrumental yearnings of the corporations. The goal of increased profits for the corporation actively interferes with the critical analysis of TV ads. The competitive stance of the firm structures the discourse of market research into the position of the rational subject: the world appears as a mute other than is to be pushed that way or pulled this way. The only question is which configuration of images will do the best job. The position of the firm structures knowledge as a neutral window opening onto a world of discrete interacting objects. The subject remains the desire of the firm and science is its procurer. If the desire of the firm is canceled, no justification remains for discourse to constitute the world as a mechanics of interacting objects, as a pullulation of causes and effects. Knowledge as a ratio or table of causes/effects is thus connected to the presumption of a rational, autonomous subject, no doubt a male one, a fantasy of desire as profit.

The question may be raised if such correlations are, in the first place, the best research strategy for understanding TV ads and if the agent who structures the discourse is best defined as one of rational autonomy. If TV ads are about mute objects moving this way or that in a Newtonian world, then perhaps the causes and effects of those movements are indeed the object of knowledge, and then perhaps also the subject, the one who transcends that world of objects, might be figured as rational and autonomous. The difficulty with this discursive position is that TV ads and their addressees are not mute objects, not particles of nature, but linguistic patterns. Therefore to treat the communication effects of TV ads as if they were objects that are subservient to the laws of mechanics simply obscures the linguistic logic of communication acts, reduces a sign system to an action system, produces the discourse of truth as the logic of the bottom line. When an individual watches a TV ad he or she is watched by a discourse calling itself science but in fact disciplining the consuming subject to the ends of rationality and profit.

Ads as Ideology

Other events occur as well. The TV ad may be taken differently, may be construed not as an economic event for the benefit of the firm, but as a sociopolitical event, one that tells about or participates in the ongoing play of forces in the field of society. There are several important variations on the theme of TV ad as social index.

TV ads may be read as signs of the time. They may be collected and assembled as pages of a book or snapshots in an album. Each page or photo is read against the social context. In this discourse, ads have themes, themes which mirror the needs or fantasies of social groups in historic eras and therefore map the contours of everyday life. If Virginia Slims cigarettes announce to women "You've come a long way, baby," while a super-chic model puffs away in a state of nonchalant abandon, then the contradictions of the 1970s are reconciled: a woman can participate in the undoing of patriarchy while remaining a very feminine boy toy. In this reading the ad reveals the social tensions of the age while offering a resolution of them. The TV ad is interpreted as a social document, a thematics of everyday life.[8] Such a thematic recognizes the linguistic character of the TV ad but does not raise the problem of interpretation at that level. Instead the interpretation of TV ads as signs of the times stresses the relation to the social context.

The relationship of the TV ad to the social context is difficult to establish. No simple formula can assure a proper connection in advance. If that were the case the ad makers would have a record of complete success. No one can predict with certainty how a TV ad will be received by the multifarious groups and classes who view it. A group of TV ads by ARCO, the oil company, associated the company with concern for the environment and with a general sense of social responsibility. Viewers might reverse the signs, seeing the ad as a cover-up for a business that pollutes the environment and places profitability above the social good. TV ads are visual texts and as such are open to multiple interpretations. The social context approach does not account for this difficulty, an omission that places the interpreter in the position of omniscience. The historian or social scientist may unselfconsciously forge the connection between the ad and the social context, between Virginia Slims and the feminist movement. In that case the writer bypasses rather than problematizes the question of interpretation, puts together one aspect of the complex, multilayered phenomenon called society with one way of seeing the TV ad.

The definition of the TV ad in relation to the social context is amenable to various political positions. A central, persistent theme in the critical literature on the TV ad is its alleged irrational manipulation of the viewer. Advertisers work for capitalists whose aim is to sell their products, a commercial transaction in which critical distance is preserved in the warning *caveat emptor*. The goal of the TV ad is to undermine the buyer's residue of rationality, transmuting the instrumental rationality of the exchange into the baser metal of desire for unnecessary consumption. In this view, one shared by many liberals and Marxists, advertisers stop at nothing to increase sales and preserve market share: in TV ads cars indicate social status, underarm deodorants fulfill revolutionary aspirations, photocopying machines promote the labor of God, airplane rides are orgiastic experiences; women's bodies are debased, wholesome values are corrupted, innocent children are victims of cupidity.[9]

While this negative reading of TV ads cannot be gainsaid, serious difficulties are raised that are not adequately addressed. First, unacknowledged antifeminist tendencies are sometimes associated with this critique. Historians of advertising discovered a shift from informative ads that presumed a rational consumer to the irrational manipulation of which the critics complain. The shift occurred in the early twentieth century. It resulted from the awareness by advertisers that women were the main consumers.[10] Advertisers assumed that women are irrational, and reshaped ads to appeal to social anxieties and romantic aspirations so as to better promote their product to a female audience. Critics implicitly blame the victim, women, in their tirade against advertising, displacing moral responsibility from the emitter of the communication to its receiver. When a man watches a TV ad, his autonomy is threatened by feminine irrationality.

Second, the critic of TV ads subliminally introduces a defense of the bourgeois male subject, the autonomous, rational ego as the foundation of the discourse. What the ads undermine, to these readers, is the autonomy of the self which is uncritically taken as a moral, political and ontological good. In liberal accounts, this defense is often straightforward.[11] In Marxist writers, the situation is more complex. A curious displacement occurs. The ideal subject as rational individual, the classic bourgeois, is appropriated by and merged into the position of the critique, while the bourgeois, now the hedonist consumer, assumes the role of destroying that ideal.[12] Incongruously,

Marxist discourse is combined with nostalgia for bourgeois subjectivity. Lears and Fox, for example, attribute to the bourgeoisie of
the Progressive Era the source of a shift from an ethos of Protestant
asceticism to a consumer culture framed as a desire for "self-
fulfillment and immediate gratification."[13] From a Marxist standpoint
this change is simply a reshuffling of ruling-class ideologies, or in
Lears's Gramscian language, a move from one "capitalist cultural
hegemony" to another.

Yet Lears's account of this change is troped as a decline. In the
new consumer culture there is a "collapse of meaning" through a
"misuse of language".[14] Advertising produces a corruption of
language: "Advertising helped to create a culture in which there
were few symbols rooted in specific customs (as in traditional
cultures), nor even many signs with specific referents (as in Victorian
culture)."[15] But why is this a "misuse"? For a Marxist, the change
from Victorian referential cultural hegemony to the twentieth
century's language of advertising is a move from one system of
domination to another, hardly a decline through misuse of language.
Like Christopher Lasch, Lears complains about the therapeutic sense
of life as continuous growth which is somehow corrosive: "Ultimately
the most corrosive aspect of the therapeutic ethos was the worship
of growth and process as ends in themselves."[16] The question of
what exactly is being eaten away is left unanswered, but it is implied
that the older bourgeois culture, with its autonomous, sacrificing,
stable male ego is the threatened object.

Lears's account is typical of much Marxist cultural critique in that
it takes the standpoint of the old bourgeoisie in order to attack the
new ruling ethos.[17] Such a move is necessarily flawed, even reaction-
ary. Instead of developing a critique of advertising rooted in language
theory, this position retreats to a defense of rationalist subjectivity,
a position from which one can only mount a moral complaint about
the present rather than being able to distinguish liberating possibilities
from structures of domination. To this sort of Marxism, the analysis
of the present conjuncture becomes a lament for an earlier capitalist
epoch even if that is not the explicit intention of the author. Without
a concept such as the mode of information, the critic is stuck between
the Scylla of advertising language and the Charybdis of bourgeois
referentiality; to condemn the former one necessarily grounds one's
position on the latter. For many male Marxists, bourgeois referential
language, rooted as it is in the subject as autonomous ego, consistently
appears the better choice. This choice rightly displeases feminists
because such a definition of the subject positions women as its

excluded other. Social critique requires categories that are beyond the Marxist framework if the language of advertising is to be addressed in a manner that avoids sexist definitions of the subject while accounting for the emergent linguistic structures of domination.[18]

My reading of Lears's analysis of the TV ad uncovers a recourse to a value (autonomy) that is not explicitly defended in his text. My justification for resorting to that value in criticizing his argument is that it alone fills in a gap or recovers an absence in his discourse. These gaps occur when he employs terms like "corrosive" or "misuse" without providing their antecedents. The reader is expected to fill in those antecedents with appropriate terms ("proper" or referential use of language for "misuse" and "rationality" for "corrosive"), terms which themselves cannot be questioned precisely because they are unnamed. The use of these terms permit Lears to present a critique of the ethos of "self-realization" in advertising against the backdrop of the earlier ethos of "salvation" without implicating his own Marxist position. The (Marxist) reader is authorized by the discourse to concur with Lears's critique without calling into question the position (Marxism relying upon referentiality) from which the critique is generated. The problem illustrated by Lears's text is that the critique of TV ads will lapse into a defense of referential discourse, itself dependent on an ontology of the rational subject, unless the critique is grounded in a language-based theory of communication.

At the overt level of textual analysis Lears's discourse refers to a Gramscian critique of bourgeois culture. Many Marxist historians are attracted to this position because it explains culture and ideology as forms of repression which are alternatives to state violence. Bourgeois society normally maintains its hegemony, argues the Gramscian position, not by resort to police repression but through the gentler rule of its ideas and cultural values. TV ads then serve to defuse the radicalism of the workers by confusing them with images of consumer self-realization. In this view TV ads are yet another mechanism of capitalist domination. A secondary benefit to the Marxist position deriving from the Gramscian concept of cultural hegemony is that the compliance of workers to capitalist society appears less embarrassing. When a worker views a TV ad, class consciousness is false.

Gramsci's theory of cultural hegemony is carried further by Althusser's theory of ideological state apparatuses. Althusser complained that Gramsci's position was "unsystematic,"[19] and attempted to correct that flaw. Althusser defines ideology as the *representation* of "the imaginary relationship of individuals to their real [productive] conditions of existence."[20] He emphasizes that his definition focuses not on the "*real* conditions of existence" but on the individual's *relationship* to those conditions.[21] The relation of the individual to those conditions is, for Althusser, always imaginary (in the Lacanian sense), an imaginary that is the basis of the "distortions" that Marx and others have noted to be characteristic of ideological discourse. Going against the grain of most Marxist positions on ideology, Althusser affirms the materiality of this imaginary by asserting its rootedness in an apparatus along with its associated practices. The ideology of advertising, for instance, is rooted in the apparatus of the advertising firm and its production facilities as well as in the system of broadcasting. In addition the "practice" of viewing TV is part of the ideology of advertising.

Althusser takes a further step by arguing that the chief effect of ideology is to constitute living individuals as subjects.[22] The TV ad viewer, then, is structured by the ad to recognize himself or herself as a consuming subject. This recognition is at once ideological and a misrecognition since the ad represents the relation of the individual to his or her "real conditions of existence" as an *imaginary* one. The ad constitutes the individual as a "subject" who is able to buy the product, as a "subject" who labors and earns income that is disposable and as a "subject" who is able freely to choose to desire the product. Properly speaking, an individual does not receive the communication of the ad unless he or she is so constituted in the practice of viewing. The individual "recognizes" himself or herself as such a subject during the viewing and *misrecognizes* his or her relation to the "real conditions of production" precisely by so recognizing himself or herself. The ideological effect of the ad is to reproduce the conditions by which the individual becomes a "subject" of capitalist society, a legally free, autonomous worker and consumer. Such a subject is of course in an imaginary relation to the capitalist mode of production, a "distorted"' relation in the sense that the subject believes him or herself to be an agent when in fact he or she is constituted by the structure as its bearer. All of this ideological practice occurs, Althusser reminds the reader, not in some public space but in the isolated "privacy" of the subject's home, far removed from the clamor of history and politics. Ideological effects thus deny that they are taking place as they occur. Nonetheless ideology may be and often is a terrain of class struggle because it is rooted in Ideological State Apparatuses, institutions that are exposed to contestation.[23] When a person views a TV ad, capitalism is either reproduced or attacked.

NeoMarxist writers like Althusser have made important contributions to understanding the TV ad in relation to a critical view of the social context. Serious difficulties, however, impair the critical value of Althusser's discourse. Althusser accounts for the specific effects of cultural practices, such as TV ads as the constitution of the subject, thereby advancing beyond Gramsci both by relating cultural hegemony to material practices and by undermining the humanist concept of the centered subject. In this way, an Althusserian analysis of TV ads is not flawed by reliance on an absent autonomous subject. Even so the problem of the subject reemerges in Althusserian discourse through the question of science.

Althusser claims scientific status for his concept of ideology. He derives the truth value of his discourse by distinguishing it from that of ideology. While ideology is a general condition of all subjects, imposing its distorting effects on everyone at all times, scientific discourse is immune from this limitation because, Althusser asserts, there is no subject of scientific discourse: "the author, insofar as he writes the lines of a discourse which claims to be scientific, is completely absent as a 'subject' from 'his' scientific discourse (for all scientific discourse is by definition a subject-less discourse, there is no 'Subject of science' except in an ideology of science) . . ."[24] In addition, his analysis of specific ideologies is not itself ideological because it adopts the standpoint of the class struggle: "It is only from the point of view of the classes, i.e. of the class struggle, that it is possible to explain the ideolog*ies* existing in a social formation."[25] This extraordinary privilege accorded to Marxist discourse only serves to constitute the Marxist theoretical subject as the bourgeois subject, the autonomous, transcendent, rational ego who is capable of undistorted knowledge.

The problem of the centered subject emerges also when Althusser claims that his discourse has access to the social totality. Marxism is a science of the whole. All other positions – feminist, anti-nuclear, gay and lesbian, anti-racist – are thereby rendered ideological since Marxism has colonized the domain of the scientific. Totalizing theories are no less repressive when they derive, as Althusser's does, from "critical" positions. In the last instance, Althusser warns, "it is the base which . . . determines the whole edifice."[26] When an Althusserian theorist views a TV ad its ideological effects are neutralized.

If the strength of the Althusserian theory of ideology stems from the relation it draws between Ideological State Apparatuses and the means of production, its weakness rests with its inability to specify the mechanisms at play in each such apparatus. In the case of the TV ad, the Althusserian position fails to elaborate, at the level of communications practice, the structural complex through which the subject is constituted. In the last instance, this is the most serious problem with his theory of ideology. In the absence of a theory of the language-effects of advertising, Althusser's position is unable to estimate the extent to which TV ads are not ideological, do not reinforce an exploitation that is situated elsewhere in the social world. Instead they initiate their own kind of difficulty, a difficulty that is not reducible to the mode of production, does not derive directly from it and cannot be redressed by changing it.

In the end, Althusser's concept of ideology, as distinct from historically rooted ideological state apparatuses, interprets all culture as extensions of the means of production. Outside of this relation, ideology is, for him, an ahistorical phenomenon. "Ideology has no history,' he writes; it is a universal, necessary mirror of misrecognition, like the Lacanian Oedipal phase, a broad, general category that reveals little about the experiences of an age. Ironically, Althusser is unable to raise what should be the historical materialist question about culture: how does a given cultural phenomenon change and how does that change generate historically distinct modes of domination? This is the question that must be raised about TV ads and more generally about electronically mediated communication. The issue of new forms of domination at the cultural level challenges Marxism for control of the terrain of historical materialism. If it can be shown that forms of domination are constituted and have their effects at the level of culture, and that these do not derive from the means of production, then Marxism, insisting on "determination in the last instance by the means of production," raises its voice *against* the comprehension of contemporary modes of domination and must be regarded as a retrogressive force.

The Sign System

The Althusserian theory of ideology shows its limitations as a critical theory when confronted with societies which are increasingly characterized by communication situations exemplified by the TV ad. The concept of ideology interprets linguistic phenomenon through the grid of representational logic. Ideological practices are indexed on the means of production; these are "objective" processes, available to scientific understanding. (Marxist) science generates concepts which represent the structure of society. Reality is centered in reason. The imaginary or the nonrational becomes an empty universal, a level of ideology that uniformly beclouds the minds of prescientific subjects. The TV ad and electronically mediated communication in general, however, have important effects through structures which are nonreferential. Ideological apparatuses, Althusser argues, constitute a centered subject which is illusory. TV ads, on the contrary, promote a decentered subject which undermines the distinction between the illusory and the real. TV ads undermine the distinction between science and ideology, true and false consciousness, the real and the imaginary. They are structures without direct referents, invented models of reality which themselves contest the distinction between the real and the fictional, strings of words and images that represent nothing but themselves.

I will attempt to sustain this argument about TV ads and the media in general by (1) critically reviewing the position of Jean Baudrillard, the individual most closely associated with this position, and (2) outlining a communications model of the TV ad as discourse/practice.

Baudrillard's thinking about the media follows a trajectory from neoMarxism to poststructuralism.[27] His early writings, from 1968 to 1973, are efforts to supplement Marxism with a theory of consumer objects. To the critique of political economy, Baudrillard adds a critique of the political economy of the sign; to the mode of production he adds the mode of signification. He analyzed consumerism from an "orthodox" New Left position: advanced capitalism shifts the social crisis of capitalism from production to consumption. The economic problem today is not how to produce an automobile but how to sell it. The analysis of consumption requires a shift from economic categories of values and utilities to linguistic categories of signs and signifiers. Baudrillard synthesized the Barthes of *Mythologies* with a Lacanian Freud: commodities generate desire by merging fantasies with banalities, the erotic and the economic. The merger is accomplished semiotically, by transforming the structure of language.

Normally a sign is composed of a word and a mental image and is associated with a referent, a "thing" in the "real" world. When signs are exchanged between individuals they become symbolic; their meaning floats ambiguously between the individuals, associated as it necessarily is with their relationship to each other. The word does not simply have a "meaning"; it is also shared between the speakers, exchanged like gifts that enrich or diminish the social tie. Such at any rate is Baudrillard's linguistic utopia, his ideal speech situation.

The advertised consumer object changes all of that. The ad takes a signifier, a word that has no traditional relation with the object being promoted, and attaches it to that object. The ad constitutes a new linguistic and communications reality. These floating signifiers derive their effects precisely from their recontextualization in the ad. Extracted from an actual relation between lovers, romance or sexiness increases in linguistic power. In the ad, the sexy floor wax is more romantic than a man or women in an actual relationship. This surplus meaning, to repeat, derives from the unique linguistic structure of the ad. Romance in the floor-wax ad is constituted by words and images that are *not found* in daily life. An attractive man abruptly appears in (penetrates into) an ordinary kitchen while an average woman futilely scrubs away using the wrong product. The very impossibility of the sexy man making his appearance in the kitchen as he does (he *pops* into the picture, for example, by virtue of a careful splice of the videotape) sets the ad apart from representational and scientific logic. The cartoon-like appearance of the man registers the image as fantasy, a fantasy of Prince Charming, but a Prince Charming who exists not in books of fiction, not in remote fairy tales, but in an image of a kitchen very much like one's own. Johnson's floor wax now equals romantic rescue. The commodity has been given a semiotic value that is distinct from, indeed out of phase with, its use value and its exchange value. The very "senselessness" of the relation romance = floor wax is a condition of its communications meaning.

Baudrillard's argument is not that people "believe" the ad; that itself would assume a representational logic, one subject to cause–effect analysis (how many people bought the product because they saw the ad). Nor is his argument based on irrational manipulation; the ad works on the unconscious of the viewer, subliminally hypnotizing the viewer to buy the product. This would be a Freudian-like reversal of the logic of representation. Instead Baudrillard sets his argument in linguistic terms: the ad shapes a new language, a new set of meanings (floor wax/romance) which everyone speaks or better which speaks everyone. Baudrillard calls the collective language of commodity ads "the code," a term which he has not adequately defined or elaborated.

The code may be understood as a language or sign system unique to the mode of information, to electronically mediated communication systems. The code speaks individuals in the same way that all language may be understood to speak individuals, as a sign system. As Saussure demonstrated long ago, the binary structure of signs, the set of semantic differences through which meaning is constituted, requires for its intelligibility that one situate the subject of speech not as an agent but as an effect of the structure of language.[28] When a speaker utters the word "I" he or she *is spoken* by English, a language in which the words I and you are differentiated to indicate distinct linguistic positions. The social effect of the ad (floor wax/romance) is not economic or psychological but linguistic: the TV viewer participates in a communication, is part of a new language system. That is all. But that is also enough to constitute a social formation. Without comprehending this language effect of ads, critical social theory cannot grasp the new structural dimensions introduced by the mode of information. The temptation must be resisted to interpret the ad by the hermeneutics of suspicion within the representational logic of Marxism which sees the ad as a "corruption" of values, an "abuse" of language. Such a strategy will miss the point, will obscure the language of the code, and will reduce its effects to those of the logic of capital.[29]

Society as a Language

Roland Barthes carried the concept of language as code one step beyond Saussure by analyzing a defined social phenomenon, fashion, as a linguistic structure. He presented an analysis of the code of fashion, vacillating between a historical and a universalist view of the language structure of fashion. The code of fashion was for him, on the one hand, related to late industrial capitalism, and, on the others, like literature, an anthropological exemplar of the symbolic. He defined fashion as follows hand;

> A kind of machine for maintaining meaning without ever fixing it, it is forever a disappointed meaning, but it is nevertheless meaning: without content, it then becomes the spectacle human beings grant themselves of their power to make the insignificant signify; Fashion then appears as an exemplary form of the general act of signification, thus rejoining the very being of literature . . . hence it becomes the sign of the 'properly Human.'[30]

He argued here that the language of the code is not a new phenomenon associated with the mode of information but an inherent possibility of all language. While his argument is to some extent

correct, it avoids making the connection between new communication
situations introduced by electronically mediated communications and
new languages like the code. The social force of the code cannot be
abstracted from these communications settings into a register of the
universals of language. To do so is to negate the historical dimension
of language, to undermine a critical social theory of the code, and,
worst of all, to constitute the theorist as subject of the universal, to
transmute the conditioned, finite author into an absolute, ahistorical
ground of knowledge. While Barthes's *The Fashion System* does not
need to be interpreted in a universalist manner, his failure adequately
to ground his analysis in historical and social contexts leaves open
that possibility.

The Fashion System goes part way toward historical analysis.
Barthes shows that fashion operates by restricting meaning, by
closing the semantic field so that variations of style are limited. Each
new style can be composed of "strong, clear, durable signs" which
can be forgotten in time for the next season. This continuous play
among signs leads not to boredom but to the elevation of fashion
itself to being a sign at a second level. One keeps up with the current
fashion in order to remain fashionable. Fashion must sustain itself
as a code and must be analyzed at the semiotic level. If fashion is
understood as manipulation to increase sales, one misses its semiotic
power. Thus "being language, sociology ultimately cannot avoid this
[semiotic level of] analysis . . ."[31]

Barthes supplements the semiotic structural analysis with a historical one. At one time restricted to the aristocracy, fashion is today
for everyone.[32] The extension of fashion required the standardization
of commodities through mass production methods. Standardized
objects somehow generate a code in which objects become their signs
(for example, the ten gallon hat = Western). Barthes never explains
this process with the rigor of Baudrillard. Instead in *The Fashion
System* and in *Mythologies*,[33] he argues that mass society "natura-
lizes" signs – that is its linguistic uniqueness. Premodern societies
only "read" nature; modern society "explains" it.[34] The language
of explanation, however, "rationalizes" the sign, makes it both
arbitrary and natural. Modern society both obscures the properly
linguistic quality of the sign and makes the commodity nothing more
than a sign. On this basis Barthes generates a metalinguistic criterion
for judging social languages: "we can then imagine defining human
societies according to the degree of 'frankness' of their semantic
systems and according to whether the intelligibility they infallibly
assign to things is frankly signifying or allegedly rational . . ."[35]

"Frankness" is achieved only in literature which denies the "natural" character of language by creating the illusion of fixed meanings while at the same time undermining those meanings. Fiction both pretends to be "true" and erases that pretense.

Barthes's analysis eludes a critical theory of language by essentializing literature. His criterion of "frankness" could be set in the mode of information to claim that TV ads are truly "frank" since they simulate their own reality and pretend to do nothing else. Far from "naturalizing" the commodity, TV ads play with its meaning. They constitute the subject as one who may play with his or her identity by taking on the various "meanings" of the commodities. The subject of TV ads is "frank" in recognizing the unfixed, unnatural, ungrounded quality of language, whereas the reader of the novel escapes from that "frankness" by being essentialized as a "cultured" subject precisely through the recognition of the fictional truth of the language of the novel. The viewer of TV ads is in no such danger. When a person watches a TV ad, language is recognized as a socially constructed play of differences.

Society as Simulation, or The Hyperreal

The historical constitution of language concerns the restructuring of the sign and the system of signs so that reality is configured differently in the communicative action of each mode of signification. With Baudrillard we can say that the mode of signification of the classical capitalist period was the representational sign.[36] The social world was constituted in the figure of "realism" through signs whose stable referents were material objects. The medium of exchange that held together signifier and signified was reason. The communicative act that best exemplified the representational sign was reading the written word. The stability and linearity of the written word help to constitute the subject in reason, a confident, coherent subject who spoke the language of realism through signs whose highest ideal was the discourse of natural science. Modes of signification are certainly not exclusive or uniform in any epoch; but an argument could be made that in the epoch preceding our own, this representation form was dominant.

In the modern period the signifier held an abstract relation to the signified. For many words were the tools of reason, having no inherent connection with the meanings they evoked or with the things to which those meanings pointed, yet still secure enough. The

metanarrative of reason underlay this mode of signification, certified
for each individual repeatedly through acts of reading, through
continuously following in the mind's eye the unidirectional flow of
printed words. The bourgeoisie lived and many continue to live
unselfconsciously in the cloud of the representational mode of
signification. The construction of the great industrial empires was
directed by those who had no doubt that words and things cohered
and represented objects, just as bricks and mortar combine to form
walls. Confronted by the morning newspaper or the ledger book,
words constituted the subject in the mode of reason, as the
instrumental subject. This adult, white, male subject surveyed the
social world from a place of transcendental freedom only to the
extent that he had already been constituted by the representational
mode of signification.

In the informational mode of signification (the mode of
information) things go differently. The abstract conventionality in
the internal relation of the components of the sign characteristic of
the earlier period is carried a giant step farther. The all-important
link between sign and referent is shattered in what Henri Lefebvre,
Baudrillard's mentor, called "the decline of the referentials."[37] The
new mode of signification is characteristic of the mass media. In
Richard Terdiman's analysis, newspapers were the first to change
from the mode of representation to the mode of information, from
contextualized, linear analysis to a montage of isolated data giving
an appearance of objectivity. But what else is so-called objectivity
than this depoliticized simulation of truth.[38] In Paris as elsewhere
newspapers changed from being organs of particular points of view
to purveyors of "all the truth that's fit to print" in the second half
of the nineteenth century at a time when circulation soared to mass
proportions. The more newspapers moved away from distinct
communities, the more disjoint they were from their reference group,
the more their discourse left the model of representation in favor of
that of information.

In TV ads, where the new mode of signification is most clearly
seen, floating signifiers are attached to commodities only in the
virtuoso communication of the ad. The ability of language to signify,
to present meaning is not simply acknowledged by recognition of
its conventionality; it becomes the subject and structure of the
communication. Each TV ad replicates in its structure the ultimate
facility of language: language is remade, new connections are
established in the TV ad through which new meanings emerge. If
the TV ad is read through the representational mode of signification,

it is interpreted as an offense, a manipulation, a set of falsehoods, deeply disgusting and even morally dangerous. And so it is as if the world is constituted with reference to the adult, white, male metanarrative of reason.

But it is difficult day after day to sustain such a reading of the TV ad and it is important to investigate why it is so difficult. As ad after ad is viewed, the representational critic gradually loses interest, becomes lulled into a noncritical stance, is bored and gradually receives the communication differently. My argument is that the ads constitute the viewer in a nonrepresentational, noninstrumental communications mode, one different from reading print.[39] Surely the TV ad is designed to sell the product but in doing so it remakes language. The instrumental function is denegated by the TV ad; the ad only works to the extent that it is not understood to be an ad, not understood instrumentally. Through its linguistic structure the TV ad communicates at a level other than the instrumental which is placed in brackets. Floating signifiers, which have no relation to the product, are set in play; images and words that convey desirable or undesirable states of being are portrayed in a manner that optimizes the viewer's attention without arousing critical awareness.

A communication is enacted, in the TV ad, which is not found in any context of daily life. An unreal is made real, a set of meanings is communicated that have no meaning. In Baudrillard's terms a simulation of a communication is communicated which is more real than reality.[40] The commodity-object in the TV ad is not the same as the one taken home from the store and consumed. The latter is useful but prosaic, efficient but forgettable, operational but ordinary. The object in the ad and in the store display is magical, fulfilling, desirable, exciting. The difference between the two is produced by the TV ad in its communication which constitutes the subject within the code. The hyperreal is linguistically created in the TV ad; it vanishes when the consumer becomes a user, when the subject constituted by the communication becomes a subject constituted in the everyday relation to the commodity-object.

Or perhaps not, perhaps the simulation effect continues. Baudrillard contends that the hyperreal is our "reality," not just in TV ads but as the way in which late twentieth-century culture mobilizes subjects. *"It is reality itself today that is hyperrealist. . . .* Today it is quotidian reality in its entirety – political, social, historical and economic – that from now on incorporates the simulatory dimension of hyperrealism. We live everywhere already in an 'esthetic' hallucination of reality."[41] The generalization of the concept of the hyperreal from specific

communications practices to the social totality is the problematic
element in Baudrillard's discourse, the aspect of his position that the
critical theory of the mode of information must reject. At this point
in Baudrillard's position a differential analysis of a set of discourses/
practices recedes in favor of global statements. Such statements as
"We live everywhere already . . ." make claims that are beyond the
limit of the situated finitude of their author.

As one Marxist critic, Gerry Gill, has pointed out, "Baudrillard
grants to the 'code' an almost total sway across economy, politics,
ideology and culture . . ."[42] He favorably compares Althusser's
position to that of Baudrillard: "Where, for Althusser, ideology
constitutes persons as subjects, for Baudrillard signs and the code
assign subjects to their places in an hierarchical social order and
locks them into a discourse which allows only commodity and sign
exchange."[43] Gill's Marxism permits him to condone Baudrillard's
early critique of commodities as a valuable supplement to historical
materialism, but to reject the more recent work as the "ideology"
of poststructuralism. Like the poststructuralists, Gill complains,
Baudrillard abstracts from the "intersubjective moment" and then
"revels in the experience of active de-centered subjectivity."[44] The
Althusserian Marxist critique of poststructuralism contextualizes this
"active de-centered subjectivity."

Poststructuralists practice a reading of texts in which meaning is
actively constituted by the reader. The practice of the intellectual by
which the self is constituted in isolated readings, Gill argues, has
been extended by capitalism to all of mass society by the generalization
of higher education. Mass education means "training in thinking
hypothetically and systematically about the world [and] requires that
the ego separate itself from identification with particular pre-given
roles and norms of closed group life."[45] The poststructuralists thus
theorize a new social practice, but their mistake, he claims, is that
they omit the self-reflexive moment whereby their own practice is
contextualized. Gill critically concludes that the "poststructuralist
and deconstructionist project is a commitment to the social condition
which generate and maintain its distinctive mode of subjectivity . . . while masking its constitutive conditions . . ."[46]

While this critique of poststructuralism may apply in some degree
to Derrida, Barthes, Lacan and perhaps others, it is not germane to
the position of Baudrillard. The theorist of the hyperreal is constantly
at pains to capture those practices through which his position is
generated. Few theorists are more self-reflexive than Baudrillard. His
writing is bathed in a sense of the social reality around him and

betrays a continuing effort to clarify his own experience in relation to that social present. Baudrillard's is not a case of the world being confined to the edges of the book. In fact, by implying that the mode of information is structured by the practice of reading, the Marxist critic is off target. The TV ad is not like reading, does not follow the linear logic of representation. One could argue the opposite: the spread of the hyperreal in TV ads and the like creates a practice of self-constitution that becomes translated by poststructuralists like Derrida, Foucault and Barthes into a new practice of reading, one that violates the traditional mode of signification associated with reading, one that breaks with the literalness and stability, the monolithic univocality of the printed word. If anything poststructuralists translate reading practices through the language of the mode of information. Precisely this may explain the violent opposition they arouse in so many quarters: they have transgressed the rules of representational discourse associated with the book, bringing to reading the vertiginous multivocality of the TV ad. Gill may be right that Derrida is not reflexive about the sociolinguistic context of his discourse, but he is wrong to define that discourse as one of reading. Deconstruction may better be defined as TV viewing applied to books. It takes the substanceless unreality of the TV ad as the metanarrative of writing.

The Marxist critique of the hyperreal is an ambiguous one. On one side the hyperreal is recognized as an increasingly dominant ideological moment; on the other it is condemned as an ideological misconstruction. One cannot have it both ways: either Baudrillard has got it wrong and the hyperreal does not correspond to practices of self-constitution in contemporary society, or something is at play in Baudrillard's position that uncovers an important feature of society, one that cannot be accounted for from within the categories of the mode of production, one whose articulated complexity requires discursive strategies that are antithetical to Marxism. The Marxist's ambivalence is revealed when he both condemns the self-absorption of poststructuralists and also affirms that they extend the freedom of the individual beyond "all prior limits of human existence."[47] The "peak experience" of reading in which the individual constitutes himself or herself by defining the meaning of the text also applies, Gill laments, to acts of consumption. But that is the "contradiction" of the mode of information: it promises a new level of self-constitution, one beyond the rigidities and restraints of fixed identities, but also makes possible the subordination of the individual to manipulative communications practices. The alternative is not to

The TV Ad and the Mode of Information

In the mode of information a new set of language/practice is imposed on existing ones, those in face-to-face and print contexts. The TV ad is the extreme tendency of the media region of the mode of information: it is a monologic, self-referential communication with asynchronous speech contexts. The means of communication are removed from the community of speakers and are abstracted from their material base in the mode of production. New technologies of transmitting at a distance are a necessary condition for this abstraction, but they do not determine the internal structure of the signs. The new language/practice is a cultural creation, one without an authorial center, but one related to the mode of production and to the field of forces in which it appears.

The TV ad as sign system holds an ambiguous relation to the project of emancipation. It incorporates the subject into itself as a dependent spectator, constituting the subject as a consumer. But in so doing it dissolves the autonomous subject, the rational male bourgeois. As a language/practice the TV ad undermines the type of subject previously associated with the capitalist mode of production and with the associated forms of patriarchy and ethnocentrism. Though it substitutes the subject as spectator/consumer it also deconstructs the subject as a centered, original agent. In order to communicate a message to a receiver, under the conditions of asynchronous monologue, the TV ad constitutes itself as language/world with the receiver in the position of the referent. The receiver/consumer is the god who guarantees that the TV ad "works" or has "meaning." Only the absent recipient of the message can guarantee that the language of the TV ad is spoken well.

The receiver of the message thus plays two roles, one as manipulated, passive, consumerist *object* of the discourse, another as judge, validator, referent *subject* of the discourse. Constituted as both object and subject, thing and god, the viewer is presented with the impossibility of the position of the subject, the basic insubstantiality of the subject. To "read" the TV ad, to find meaning in it requires a double positioning: one must *accept* the illocutionary force of the message (buy the product); one must also *create* the meaning of the ad (*make* the sign) by attaching the floating signifier to the signified product. The simultaneous, disjunctive position of the viewer unsettles the illusory solidity of the constituted subject. In the TV ad a language has been made which leaves/urges viewers to regard their own subjectivity as a constituted structure, to regard themselves as members of a community of self-constituters, an asynchronous community separated in space and time (with VCRs, satellites), a mute community, a community of individuals who participate in the self-referential conversation of the TV ad in one manner only: by constituting themselves as subject/object of the message.

To the extent that TV ads (and, tendentially, the media in general) constitute subjects as self-constituters, the hegemonic forms of self-constitution are put into question. Conversations that are structured undemocratically, talks between bosses and workers, men and women, whites and nonwhites, adults and children, reinforce hegemonic forms of self-constitution in which a subject is both subordinate and fixed. Thus the "other side" of TV ads is their threat to these discourses/practices, a threat that may have little direct political impact at this time, but nonetheless may be an opening to a critique of the languages of domination. TV ads and, more generally, the media region of the mode of information extend the domain of unfreedom by the linguistic constitution of consumer subjects and open discourse to a new level of freedom by deconstructing all forms of centered subjects.

3

Foucault and Databases

Participatory Surveillance

All information in all places at all times.

From *Gutenberg Two*

TV Ads and Databases

In the TV ad a new language situation is structured by the manipulation of context, the reduction of conversation to monologue, and the self-referentiality of the message. The database represents a somewhat different language situation. In this case the individual is not addressed at all; he or she receives no messages. Rather the communication goes the other way round. The individual, usually indirectly, sends messages to the database. In one sense the database is nothing more than a repository of messages. As a form of language it resembles the earliest uses of writing: collections of data about some aspect of daily life.[1] As in the case of TV ads, however, the electronic mediation of a language situation changes everything. In this chapter I will analyze stored language in the mode of information, in computer jargon, databases. The structure of databases and their relation to society are best disclosed by reference to the work of Michel Foucault, in particular his analysis of discourse. The linguistic quality of the database, its implications for politics, can best be captured by a theory, like Foucault's, that problematizes the interdependence of language and action.

Harbinger of the Absolute Subject

Enthusiasts of information society loudly herald an era of perfect communication. Godfrey and Parkhill proclaim: "All information in all places at all times. The impossible ideal. But the marriage of computers with existing communications-links will take us far closer to that goal than we have ever been."[2] The authors of *Gutenberg Two* evoke what is increasingly becoming a central emblem of futurists: in the comfort of home, seated before a computer equipped with a modem, the individual has access to all the information in all the world's databanks. One is reminded of Flaubert's farcical portrayal of this search for total, perfect knowledge. Two of his characters, Bouvard and Pécuchet, futilely amass and arrange all truths. Sartre, in *Nausea*, presented a negative character who resolutely read an entire library, starting from A and proceeding to Z, in a similar quixotic quest. The more contemporary fantasy assumes the following:

1 that the entire printed corpus is digitally encoded and stored;
2 that no resulting "library" is "password protected," or in the lingo of old-fashioned capitalism, "private";
3 that individuals will use such information and that this use has no political implications; and
4 that nothing significant is lost in the process of digital encoding, storage, retrieval, transmission and reproduction.

Each of these assumptions is highly suspect.

Keeping Tabs

First, the digital encoding of printed records is indeed proceeding apace. The number and extent of databases is large and rapidly increasing. No one who has looked at the statistics on databases or confronted its reach can fail to be astounded. David Burnham, writing in 1983, states: "The five largest credit reporting companies in the United States maintain in their computers more than 150 million individual credit records."[3] In that same year it happened that I bought a car. Prior to signing the contract, the dealer routinely ran a TRW credit check on me. Before my eyes, sitting in a place I had never been with a salesperson I had never met, in a few seconds a list of all my credit transactions spewed from a printer, including education loans and minor matters I had long ago forgotten. Though seen today as a technically trivial accomplishment, the credit check graphically illustrates the ominous meaning of "All information in all places at all times."

In addition to credit companies, databases are maintained by health insurance companies, municipal police, state motor vehicle agencies, innumerable federal bureaus, banks, utility companies – the list goes on and on. Back in 1974 in a study of record keeping in major institutions, James Rule concluded that databases enable the detailed reconstitution of the daily activities of any individual.[4] In addition to becoming more extensive, databases have added new capabilities. They now may include color pictures as well as text so that the identification of persons or things is facilitated. Records may be transferred to permanent, miniature ROM chips in which form, for example, such "Life Cards" may be worn on the wrist and contain an individual's medical history in case of emergency.[5] In addition databases are easily interconnected, constituting a vast network of stored information about the populace that must rival the infinite account books of Heaven.[6]

Confronted by such a massive intrusion on individual privacy, legislators have vainly hustled to keep pace with the dissemination of information technology. The Privacy Act of 1974, together with the Freedom of Information Act, regulates databases kept by the federal government. The law restricts the kind of information that may be stored, narrowly limits its use to the purpose for which it was gathered, and forbids the selling of mailing lists in certain circumstances. It also permits individuals to review records kept on them. But this Act does not cover states, municipalities, or private agencies like banks and, what is most disturbing, it fails to establish an agency to enforce the law.[7] The Privacy Act raises a general social problem of the mode of information: dramatic changes in the reproduction, transmission, storage and retrieval of information profoundly affect the entire social system. Drastic changes in the means and relations of communication are making a shambles of the delicate balance in the social order that was negotiated and struggled over during the epochs of nineteenth-century industrial capitalism and twentieth-century welfare statism. Relations between national and local governments, between these and economic, educational, religious, media and familial institutions, between all of these and individuals, in short the entire social infrastructure must be recalibrated and synchronized to the databases of the mode of information.

Yet skeptics might point out that much gathering and storing of information remains to be done, and that the generation of new information continues to render Sisyphean if not ridiculous the burden of data entry. Nevertheless by imposing strict parameters on the definition of information, digital encoding greatly enhances the efficiency of the transmission and reproduction of information. If the Judeo-Christian Bible is 1,800 printed pages and there is a copy of it in a database connected to telephone lines, a person equipped with a 9,600 baud rate modem can make a copy of it in ten minutes, whereas a medieval monk, with parchment, ink and quill, produced perhaps one Bible in a year of labor. Digital encoding and electronic manipulation of language, images and sounds nullify the temporal and spatial limits of communication. Reproduction of information is exact, transmission is instantaneous, storage is permanent, and retrieval is effortless. The Enlightenment dream of an educated society, wherein all knowledge is available to the least individual, is now technically feasible. The dark world the philosophers loathed, where priests babbled in an unknown tongue, where kings and courtiers decided in private among themselves the fate of society, where merchants and artisans kept secret their methods of production and distribution of goods, that shadowy world with restricted information flows is seemingly gone forever. A new day has certainly dawned in human history, but what that day forebodes is far from clear.

Making a Buck

The database may be the condition for the possibility of a truly educated populace but technological determinists are alone in believing it will happen. New gadgets are developed in the context of existing needs, shaped by perceptions of situated individuals; they are restricted in their production and dissemination by ruling powers, and resisted by hegemonic cultural patterns and individual fears. The fact that it is technically possible for information to be available to everyone at little cost in no way ensures that it will be. In fact under the aegis of private property all efforts are made to ensure that it is not available. In the era of industrial capitalism social and natural resources essential to the production of material goods came under the control of self-interested private individuals. In the era of the mode of information the process is at work again. We are now being convinced that "information" is first a commodity and second that it is properly controlled by market forces. Capitalist economics assumes that resources are scarce and therefore that their allocation is best determined by market mechanisms. Yet information is not scarce but plentiful and cheap. In the mode of information the market inverts itself: by restricting the flow of information it produces the scarcity that economists tell us is a fact of nature.

The problem is that information is too easily reproduced. Until now commodities were difficult to reproduce. A complex combination of materials and skills were required to make almost everything. Producer and consumer were separated by the process of production. Clothing, appliances, furniture – few consumers imagined they could provide these for themselves.[8] Books, music and film were no different. Consumers paid for the manufacture of the book, not for the information in it which was available at no cost in public libraries. The same was true for phonogaph recordings: the black disc was the commodity for which one paid, not the tune it contained which could be sung by anyone. Information was inseparable from the "packages" in which it was delivered and the package had a price tag. The new technologies for reproducing information have changed all of that: photocopying devices, audio and video recorders, computer disk drives, and satellite receivers make every consumer into a producer. Anyone can reproduce information in a package that is equal to and in some cases better than the commercial package.

The principle of private property is threatened in the domain of information. New communication technologies enable people to control both the reproduction and the distribution of information. The first time one watches a television program that one has recorded on a video cassette recorder one is disoriented by the control one has over the program. The consumer only realizes how dependent he or she was on the timetable of broadcasters when the taped reproduction is stopped, fastforwarded, reversed, replayed, put into slow motion, and edited all at the convenience of the viewer. Law suits were brought against Sony for enabling this alleged violation of free enterprise. The networks lost the suit because no material damage could be proved. The courts concluded that as long as the consumer does not mass produce and market his or her video tape, no law of the market has been abrogated. The suit reveals that what the capitalists wanted was not only control of the airwaves and the content of what is sent on them, but also control of the viewer, control over when he or she watches, what is watched, the order in which it is watched, and the speed of the images. Video recorders do not really change what is viewed; they undermine the control and discipline of the viewer by the broadcaster.[9]

Video recordings and even more so audio recordings are better done by the consumer than by the producer. One can cheaply purchase better quality blank tapes than those used by the producers to make prerecorded cassettes. The home recordist dubs or copies in "real" time rather than by speeding up the process as the corporations do, resulting in a better copy, one that contains more of the information from the original than is available on commercial copies. The consumer also makes better copies by maintaining the equipment through simple cleaning of the tape path, an easy practice for the individual but one which the exigencies of mass production render difficult. Audio and video tape manufacturers use inferior tape, take too little time to make copies, and do not maintain copying equipment in optimal condition. As a consequence, in the mode of information the consumer often makes better products than the producer and does so at less cost to himself or herself. In yet another way the mode of information disrupts the practices of industrial capitalist society.

The most extreme cases of this reversal occur with digitized information. Once sounds and images are digitally encoded they may be reproduced perfectly and indefinitely. The effort to commodify information comes up against an invisible brick wall of digital reproduction. When sounds, images and language are digitally encoded they are taken out of the register of material being. The laws of inertia and conservation of energy, while not technically violated, are in practice set aside. The transformation of information from analog into digital form makes possible its transformation from naturally organized matter into manipulable electrons. In the case of language, the alphabet is reduced to a binary code of combinations of 0s and 1s (American Standard Code for Information Exchange, ASCII). Once this is accomplished electric pulses replace 0s and 1s. After this point the natural, material limits of spoken and written language no longer hold. Vast quantities of language may now be stored, transmitted or copied almost instantaneously. And since that is the case, digitized language is poorly suited to the commodity form. Digitally encoded language – computer programs, encyclopedias, books, bank records, and so forth – are susceptible to copying and also to corrupting. It appears that during the epoch of industrial society the relationship of capitalism to language required a certain complex combination by which language could only be reproduced if it was transformed into the heavy, inert shapes of matter that capitalism was preeminently designed to control. Once this arrangement was broken by electronically mediated communication devices, capitalism lost its ability to control language and it did so at the same moment that it became dependent upon language in the processes of production (science), consumption (advertising) and control (market research, systems theory, cybernetics, game theory, etc.).

Of course the system of private enterprise does not easily surrender to the liberatory potentials of historical circumstances. Every effort is made to commodify information, regardless of how inappropriate, unlikely, ludicrous, or inequitable are the consequences. Home networking, a new technology in which vast information services become available to the home computer, illustrates the problem of the commodification of information. Home networking provides the consumer with videotext information about products and the ability to order them all through the computer. These services have been available in France since the mid-1980s and are being developed in the United States.[10] On the one side, vast databases are made available to the consumer in the convenience of the home. On the other side, new databases are generated each time the consumer orders a product, thereby providing detailed information about the consumer to the corporations. As Kevin Wilson observes,

> The return channel in an interactive system . . . will . . . transmit back to industry much relevant information about consumer demand and consumption. This information will include the consumer's identity, the time and place of consumption . . . and product characteristics. This data . . . will generate an invaluable portrait of consumer activity for marketing purposes. These systems will create a truly cybernetic cycle of production and consumption; because every consumptive activity will generate information pertinent to the modification of future production.[11]

In the home networking information loop, one database (product information) generates another database (consumer information) which generates another database (demand information) which feeds the production process. In this context, the commodification of information creates its own system of expanded reproduction: producers have databases about consumers which are themselves commodities that may be sold to other producers. In the excited frenzy of the new marketing system, social critics remind us, participants often forget that computers, at the onset of the 1990s, are not yet widely available in the home in the United States. In France, however, the telephone company solved this problem by providing computers to homes with telephones in place of directories. In the long run this policy was cost effective and, more significantly, made possible the extremely lucrative service of consumer information or home networking.

Talk, Print and Electrons

The distinction between speech and writing has been gaining attention in the social sciences and the humanities just at the moment when both forms of communication are being overshadowed by electronic media. In philosophy the battle has raged between Searle's speech act theory and Derrida's concept of *écriture*. In social theory Habermas, though claiming to be badly misunderstood, has celebrated "the ideal speech situation" as the nodal point of a general, totalizing theory of communicative action. Anthony Giddens also employs a concept of "talk" as a defense against structuralist and poststructuralist critiques of the subject. Jack Goody, in *The Domestication of the Savage Mind*, defends the complexity of oral culture against the limitations of print.[12] In the case of Harold Innis, a pioneer of the history of communications, the important distinction is made between writing and print.[13] Marshall McLuhan and his followers probably remain in the minority in distinguishing between electronic and pre-electronic media.[14]

The analysis of databases in the mode of information requires an understanding of the issues at stake in these discussions of oral and print cultures. If social theory and history are to begin to take seriously the proliferation of databases and their impact on society, the rigid distinction between oral and written forms of language must be unsettled. The oral/written dichotomy obscures the uniqueness of electronic language by subsuming it under the category of writing. The questions that need to be raised are:

1 What are the ways by which electronic language (in this case databases), as distinct from speech and writing, enable and limit the transmission or storage of meaning?
2 How do the distinct social characteristics of electronic language shape the use and impact of databases?

In this discussion my purpose is not to celebrate the "victory" of electronic media over books, nor to lament the moral decay caused by electronic language. Instead I hope to contribute to a critical understanding of an emerging social formation.

The difficulties in comparing electronic language to speech and writing are illustrated in the recent work of Anthony Giddens. A leading sociological theorist, Giddens has long advocated a theory of the subject that is associated with the work of ethnomethodologists such as Garfinkel, Cicourel and Goffman. This tendency in social theory is known for its sensitivity to the complexity of the social agent's linguistic and epistemological negotiation through everyday life. Giddens astutely recognizes a dangerous blindness in the works of Marx, Weber and Durkheim to the epistemological achievements of the ordinary individual. The works of the grand social theorists betray an attachment to the Platonic distinction between knowledge and opinion. Knowledge is the outcome of theory and science; opinion is the degraded form of information available to the social agent. By implication the social agent is unconscious of the forces that control his or her destiny and incapable of attaining the truth.

To Giddens the consequences for critical social theory of such arrogance is a flawed theory of social action. Social theory is forced to waver between outright determinism and a romantic concept of the revolutionary subject, the group or individual who magically transcends the conditions of everyday life in an apocalyptic gesture of self-overcoming. If on the contrary the social agent is already understood as accomplishing a great deal in the normal course of action, the divide between freedom and determinism, subject and structure no longer yawns so widely. If commonplace activity requires linguistic subtlety and epistemological self-reflection, social agents are already capable of critical reflection. Thereby a chief obstacle in theorizing change is eliminated (the change from false to true consciousness) and the privileged status of theoretical discourse is called into question (ordinary action presupposes critical theory). The critique of the theoretical subject suggested by this revaluation of the ordinary social agent, however, remains at the implicit level in Giddens's work.

In addressing the distinction between speech and writing, Giddens prefers the term "talk" to that of "speech" because, he argues, talk suggests social activity. Talk for him is rooted in the daily intercourse of human beings in concrete contexts. Language is thereby firmly anchored in social reality and its complexity is connected not with its internal structure but with the intricate arrangements of contextual interactions. The important implication of Giddens's position is that writing lacks the complexity of situated talk. The interpretation of texts, he contends in an important statement, "occurs without certain elements of the mutual knowledge involved in co-presence within a setting, and without the co-coordinated monitoring which co-present individuals carry on as part of ongoing talk."[15] The emphasis on writing, as found for example in deconstruction, is unsuited to social theory not because, as many have argued, Derrida has no way to get beyond the text but because the model of writing, when imposed on social action, systematically misrecognizes it, overlooking its contextual complexity and richness. The expert reader of texts, when confronted with the task of interpreting ordinary speech, looks in the wrong places. Textual complexity is different from verbal complexity.

Whatever the strengths of Giddens centering of social theory on talk as opposed to writing, there is one difficulty that is particularly bothersome in relation to the theory of the mode of information. The theory of the talking agent obscures the profusion in contemporary society of language practices which include no talking agents, language practices such as the database. The model of talk is particularly unsuited to the analysis of all such important phenomena. Moreover Giddens's concern to acknowledge the talking subject leads him to dismiss all forms of electronic language as simply more instances of texts. He notes in passing that, while texts are the principal form of language that is not talk, "in modern times we have to add media of electronic communication."[16] The electronic media are thus included in the broad category of all cultural objects exclusive of speech, among which texts are pre-eminent. The case of Giddens illustrates a difficulty with the recent discussions of language: they focus on the binary opposition speech/writing thereby overlooking the distinctive importance of electronic language.

The issue is not the strength of the arguments of the defenders of each position: certainly *écriteuristes* like Derrida have made their case for the non-identity of textual meaning; certainly *talkists*, if I may be permitted so awkward a term, like Giddens and Habermas have raised our consciousness about the complexity of speech in everyday life. Both groups it seems to me have badly missed the mark in their selection of the crucial aspect of language experience. Precisely what characterizes advanced societies in the twentieth century is the emergence of new language experiences that are electronically mediated, fitting easily into the parameters of neither speech nor writing. A great deal can be understood about the speech/writing debate if it is contextualized in relation to the emergence of electronic languages. A digression is appropriate at this point on the topic of the sociolinguistic conditions of the emergence of language as the pre-eminent concern of social and literary theory.

On the talkist side, I will limit the discussion to the tradition of critical social theory. The rebels of May '68 in France raised the cry of "*la parole*" over "*le langue*," speech over "language" (understood in the structuralist sense of a network of internal binary oppositions). For the previous decade French intellectuals had moved away from Marxism and existentialism in favor of language-centered theories, away from theories that addressed the question of a free subject toward theories that exposed the internal complexity of structures. During the days of May '68, with the streets of Paris alive with conversing people, those intellectuals who had felt displaced by the wave of structuralist thought (Henri Lefebvre and Edgar Morin, for example) now pointed to the festival of talk as evidence that revolution was still possible, that the subject might still be the agent of history, that the context of a free community of co-present, self-monitoring talkers dissolved the constraints of unconscious structures.[17] Faced with the irrefutable festival of May, Lévi-Strauss, the leading structuralist anthropologist, sadly announced the end of structuralism. What is noteworthy in these first reactions to the halcyon days of May is that the temporary emergence of popular community was misrecognized by the left as proof of the inadequacies of the structuralist definition of language. Looking back to those events I see instead a transitory rupture in the historic neutralization of opposition in advanced societies, a rupture that proves nothing either way about structuralist theory but instead points to the ability of contemporary society to forestall massed street gatherings or any para-institutional collective speech act. In other words, the events of May '68 indicate by their *exceptional* character the power of the mode of information, of electronically mediated language, to subdue collective conversations in a context of social change, what Habermas calls "the public sphere."

The tradition of Giddens and Habermas privileges talk as a ground of free action. Giddens shows how talk, when it occurs in specific contexts of social interaction, necessarily includes a moment of outward and inward directed criticism. Habermas shows that "communicative action" necessarily includes validity claims that require an Enlightenment-like social individual, one who can autonomously yet collectively judge rightness, know truth, and feel compassion. In both cases spoken language contains the conditions for the possibility of an emancipated society created by and composed of free, rational individuals. While the Giddens/Habermas position is no doubt part of the story of the relation of language and society, it deflects attention from the emergent and generally prevailing language condition. What typifies advanced society is not so much the opposite of justice, truth and compassion, but language situations which operate at a different register from that of co-present, contextual self-monitoring talk or the ideal speech situation. The theoretical/political problem today is not to conceptualize the conditions of free speech but to account for the way actual language situations contain structures of domination and potentials for emancipating change. The historico-ontological possibility of free speech does nothing to nullify the actuality of electronic language. Thus the cry "la parole" in May '68, along with its theoretical elaboration by Giddens and Habermas, signals Hegel's owl of Minerva: the moment is passed when language practices are subject to the old contestatory oppositions. The factory site, with its massed, impoverished workers, no longer presents, for so many reasons, the opportunity of revolutionary talk. If contestatory language is to emerge today, it must do so in the context of TV ads and databases, of computers and communications satellites, not in a culture of co-present talk or consensual debate.

The other side, the *écriteuristes*, also have strong arguments and also misrecognize the situation. As the months and years passed after May '68, neither the structuralist position nor the pre-structuralist or existential Marxist position could be revivified. Instead a curious *mélange* of positions known as poststructuralism, one which has increasing currency in the United States if nowhere else, emerged as dominant. For the purposes of this discussion I want to call attention only to one aspect of the poststructuralist position: its focus on the written text. To gain some perspective, it is necessary first to contextualize. There are only two social groups in advanced society who by their daily practice are encouraged to regard texts as having transcendent primacy in human experience: orthodox rabbis and academicians in the humanities and some of the social sciences. It behooves these groups, if they are to avoid the dangers of myopic self-universalization, to be wary of regarding their own practice as a model for all humanity. The all-too-human tendency to see the world through one's narrow, familiar setting is a recurrent temptation that is certainly not limited to people of the book.

More seriously, perhaps, the poststructuralist argument for the centrality of the text is of course not literal. The model of writing as non-identity or *différance*, not the physical or symbolic quality of books, is the focus of the deconstructers, discourse analysts and semio-schizo-psychoanalysts. Poststructuralists want to get beyond all forms of reductionist, totalizing interpretations of texts. For them texts are not homogeneous, linear bodies of meaning; they are not expressions of authorial intention or reflections of class position. Texts distance the author from the reader, inserting an all-important space that permits acts of interpretation to set aside the hovering authority of the writer and allows one to read the text as it is laid out in printed pages. The distribution of symbols in ink on paper admits the discovery of gaps in the constellation of meaning which in turn refer, by their strategic placement, to unacknowledged hierarchies, in Nietzsche's terms, of a will to power, of yea saying and nay saying. Authors thus say more than they want to by encoding their table of values but also less than they want to by leaving fissures and gaps in the flow of their argument. The meaning of texts, for poststructuralists, results as much from the act of reading as from the act of writing, and, that being so, the diversity of readers leads to the conclusion that texts have multiple, even infinite, meanings. Finally poststructuralists maintain that experience in general, not just texts and not just language, must be understood according to this model of interpretation.

The poststructuralist argument is then that the world is not filled with acts and things each of which has one meaning, one possible interpretation. Language in that case does not represent an extralinguistic reality because inherent in all language is the non-identity of writing. No set of phrases about the world contains the truth of the world and, to make matters more complex, the world itself contains, among other things, texts. The central quest of the Western philosophical tradition (Derrida thinks since Plato, but certainly since Descartes) for final truth, truth that is certain, unconditionally grounded outside space and time, truth that is "clear and distinct" – this goal, one that is concurrent with and implicated in the domination by Europe of the rest of the planet, is nothing more than a convenient mystification, a sign of a certain will to power.

Confronted by the stunning poststructuralist subversion of fundamental assumptions, I am once again reminded of the peculiar operations of Hegel's owl. The poststructuralist intervention emerges after the great age of print, after the classical period of representationalist thought, even after the era of self-certainty in the natural sciences. Surely it was the century between the Congress of Vienna and the Treaty of Versailles in which the broad élite in the West held firmly to the great metanarratives of reason, science and progress. Transparent reality, univocal meaning, perfect representation, a stable sense of the separation of self and world – these are the hallmarks of bourgeois culture in the Age of Victoria. The dominance of printerly textuality as a language form was in that age accompanied by the very positions the poststructuralists deny. The peculiar thing about poststructuralism is that it asserts a form of interpretation rooted in writing at a time when print is being displaced or at least supplemented by electronic language, and it characterizes interpretation in the nonlinear, non-identical terms that are encouraged by the mode of information not by the print media. Confusion over just where reality is and what it might mean are the likely accompaniments not of a bourgeois reading public but of a mass viewing audience, one quietly monitored by the silent accumulation and processing of gigabytes of data.

The strength of the poststructuralist position then corresponds not to the force of writing over speech but to the penetration of the world of everyday life by electronically mediated language. The value of poststructuralist theory is its suitability for the analysis of a culture saturated by the peculiar linguisticality of electronic media. With this discussion in mind we may return to the task of analyzing the communication form of databases. The first step will be a clarification of the groups of terms (1) talk, speech act, oral culture; (2) print, writing; and (3) electronic media. The next step will be an explication of Foucault's theory of discourse in relation to databases.

The Oral, the Written and the Electronic

To many analysts there appears to be a linear historical trajectory in the relation between oral, written and electronic language: speech, followed by writing and print, followed by the electronic encoding first of sound, then of voice, then of image. In addition to this diachronic analysis a synchronic analysis shows the three forms of language to have a linear relation to space and time coordinates. At any given moment, a change from speech to writing to electronics increases the space the linguistic act can cover and decreases the time that it takes to transmit. The history of language usage appears strictly to conform to progressivist views of human development. The language forms (1) were introduced one after another, and (2) each makes the communication act increasingly more "efficient." Thus the analysis of language in human affairs appears to refute the poststructuralist assertion of the need for language-based theory. The history of communication appears to lend itself to a type of analysis that is anathema to poststructuralism. The history of communication is representable, from this point of view, as a totalizing, continuous, progressive evolution. This history supports the Enlightenment view of man as a rational ghost in a machine who gradually masters his environment and submits it to his own ends. The history of human language is one of thoughts and actions, where Odyssean man invents and struggles his way into a communications Elysian field of "all information in all places at all times."

Such is certainly the spirit of many writers who become captivated by the considerable achievements of the electronic media. One liberal writer refers to these media in his title as "Technologies of Freedom." For him, nothing less than the fate of mankind is at stake: "The easy access, low cost, and distributed intelligence of modern means of communication are a prime reason for hope."[18] In the socialist camp similar arguments abound. Claims are posited that "the combination of computers and [electronic] communications . . . eliminates centralization by opening bureaucracies to inspection and criticism by individuals."[19] Both positions theorize the mode of information with the same concepts and assumptions about the historical field that previously were employed in the analysis of political, legal, religious, and economic transformations. My argument, on the contrary, is that the introduction of new methods of communication require for their analysis language-based theories; that the representationalist assumptions of earlier historico-social theory no longer serve in the new context.

When communications are understood as a choice of speech and writing, the presence or absence of all parties in the interaction is normally the distinguishing feature. Speech is communication in the presence of the transmitter and receiver of the message; writing is communication in the absence of one party. Speech is associated with small-scale communities like tribes, villages and high-density urban neighborhoods. The introduction of writing and then print is typically viewed as a condition for the development of cognitive skills. Written texts encourage critical thinking, this argument contends, because the reception of the message occurs without the persuasive physical presense of the author, because the linear arrangement of words on consecutive pages somehow corresponds to cause and effect logic, because writing enables the isolated reception of the message and thereby promotes cool contemplation not impulsive passion, because the written page is material and stable, allowing repeated receptions of the message, and thereby affords an opportunity for reflective reconsideration, because writing undermines the authority of tradition and the legitimacy of hierarchy. The logical conclusion of this point of view is that writing and print is a fundamental part of the Western experience with its values of reason, freedom, and equality, its institutions of science, democracy and capitalism or socialism.[20]

The association of writing with intelligence has found critics. Anthropologists are especially sensitive to *écriteurisme* because of its ethnocentrism. Cultures without writing appear to lack the essential features of humanity. Jack Goody, an anthropologist, has felt it necessary to point out that spoken language is as complex as writing and in some ways it is more complex. Writing, he contends, makes possible forms of language – lists, formulas, recipes – which occur rarely in speech and which are drastic simplifications and reductions. Goody writes,

> One of the features of the graphic mode is the tendency to arrange terms in (linear) rows and (hierarchical) columns in such a way that each item is allocated a single position, where it stands in a definite, permanent, and unambiguous relationship to the others ... [a table or a list] reduces oral complexity to graphic simplicity, aggregating different forms of relationship between 'pairs' into an all-embracing unity.[21]

In this interpretation, writing is less conducive to reason, freedom and equality than speech.

For the advocates of both speech and writing, language appears as but one more institution, one more form of action. A realist assumption characterizes the whole discussion: language, whether oral or written, is simply another tool. Its effects may be gauged exactly like the effects of other institutions or routinized forms of behavior. Language is a material thing in the world regardless of how one configures its characteristics. Thus written lists, like monarchies, are hierarchical, or, from the other standpoint, face-to-face speech, like democracy, elicits critical thinking. In these discussions there are no features of language that distinguish it from other social phenomena; there is nothing to cause the historian or the communications expert or the social scientist fundamentally to alter his or her theory or methodology.

The analysis of language forms based on the distinguishing feature of the presence/absence of transmitter and receiver necessarily minimizes the importance of the introduction of electronically mediated language. The latter is nothing more than an extension of the paradigm of writing. The new media – telegraph, telephone, radio, television, tape recorder, computer, communications satellite – extend, however considerably, the separation of transmitter and receiver introduced into history by writing. From my standpoint, however, the electronic media call into question the distinction between speech and writing along with its corresponding history of communications. For one may ask if the telephone for example separates transmitter and receiver or brings them together? Does a videotape of parents who live in New York, when replayed by their children in London, promote the presence or the absence of transmitters and receivers of messages? While spatial and temporal distance between transmitter and receiver does increase in the change from speech to writing, the criterion of distance loses its organizing power with the onset of the mode of information. Electronic language situations subvert the framework that empowered the category of distance in the analysis of language; they undermine the verisimilitude and analytic force of the standpoint from which statements about presence and absence could enter scientific discourse.

The mode of information initiates a rethinking of all previous forms of language. Just as, for Marx, the anatomy of apes becomes intelligible only after the evolutionary development of human beings, so language is retrospectively reconstructed from the vantage point of the mode of information. The mode of information undermines the time/space coordinates that have been employed to fix language in various contexts. It thereby opens up an understanding of language and society that has no reference in the grid of Renaissance perspective or the mimetic realism of Enlightenment reason. Subject no longer stands opposed to object, man to nature, or essence to existence. Words cannot any longer be located in space and time, whether it be the "real time" of spoken utterance in a spatial context of presence or the abstract time of documents in a bureaucrat's file cabinet and library's archive. Speech is framed by space/time coordinates of dramatic action. Writing is framed by space/time coordinates of books and sheets of paper. Both are available to logics of representation. Electronic language, on the contrary, does not lend itself to being so framed. It is everywhere and nowhere, always and never. It is truly material/immaterial.

Foucault, Discourse and the Superpanopticon

The differences between speech, writing and electronic language are amplified and clarified in relation to the theme of surveillance, a major form of power in the mode of information. The analysis of surveillance illustrates both the importance of language-based theory to and the unique role of electronic forms of language in a conceptualization of contemporary society.

Without space/time coordinates to fix the languages of everyday life, social control becomes a major problem for the dominant groups. Opposition movements might emerge, broadcast their views and instantly disappear, only to reemerge later. Cultural trends and life styles might develop and spread without the mediating manipulation of the centralized institutions. A trivial example of the subversive language structure of the mode of information took place within the confines of the computer firm IBM itself. Like many corporations IBM encourages workers to develop ideas for improving operations. In the past the ubiquitous "suggestion box" tapped the inventiveness of employees for the benefit of the firm at the trifling cost of small prizes and awards for the "best suggestion." In many cases, the suggestion box provided anonymity for the worker, if he or she chose it, in this sensitive area of the critique of the status quo. That things could be better implied that current arrangements were not optimal.

Similar practices were used at IBM,[22] with an important difference. Instead of a box, suggestions for improvement in this high tech firm could be registered by computer. Without leaving their stations and being seen going to the box, the workers could transmit their bright ideas the moment they occurred to them. Moreover, the suggestions would instantaneously circulate to all other employees. IBM management became concerned when critical messages began appearing. Instead of innocuous proposals to change the color of walls and the like, tough, angry criticisms were raised about company policy, criticisms that named names and pulled no punches. Caught in the contradiction of its own enlightened call for improvements, management could not easily abort the rising voices of dissent. What irked management most, however, was that it could not identify the critics and thereby thwart the subversive computer chatter. Insubordinate "conversations" were everywhere and nowhere.

History, it appears, is not so much dialectical as ambiguous, or perhaps confusing would be more accurate. If rebellious language is promoted by the mode of information so is omniscient domination. In association with the rise of electronically mediated languages new forms of power have emerged, structures which systematically elude the liberal concept of tyranny and the Marxist concept of exploitation. For liberals, tyranny is a political act, an exercise of arbitrary power.

For Marxists, exploitation is an economic act, the expropriation of labor power without a compensating return of value. The emergent forms of domination in the mode of information are not acts at all but language formations, complex manipulations of symbols. To be sure, tyranny and exploitation are accompanied by discourses and the Marxist concept of ideology is an early attempt to translate the pretty dressings of ruling ideas back into the naked interests of the ruling class. For Marxists and liberals, society consists of "real" social acts, forces and institutions on the one hand, the illusory, superstructural epiphenomena on the other.

In order to make intelligible the ways in which aspects of the mode of information like the database generate new structures of domination, the analysis must turn from the foundational assumptions of liberalism and Marxism, moving instead to a Foucauldean variant of poststructuralism. Foucault's concept of discourse, especially as he practiced it in the 1970s in works like *Discipline and Punish*, is framed by assumptions that are commensurate with the kinds of formations that are found in the mode of information, particularly so in the case of databases.

In *Birth of the Clinic, Discipline and Punish: the Birth of the Prison* and *The History of Sexuality*, volume 1 Foucault discovered connections between institutional reorganization and scientific disciplines. Economics, politics and ideas all have their place in the historical conjuncture but in emerging modern society practices are organized and shaped to an important degree by bodies of texts that are called sciences. Foucault gave a new, inverted, and dangerous meaning to Bacon's motto "knowledge is power:"

> in a society such as ours, but basically in any society, there are manifold relations of power which permeate, characterize and constitute the social body, and these relations of power cannot themselves be established, consolidated nor implemented without the production, accumulation, circulation and functioning of a discourse. There can be no possible exercise of power without a certain economy of discourses of truth which operates through and on the basis of this association. We are subjected to the production of truth through power and we cannot exercise power except through the production of truth.[23]

Discursive truth is essential to the operation of power in the social field. It might be noted that in the above citation as elsewhere in his writings, Foucault never adequately clarifies the specific relation between discourse and modern society.

Max Weber also underscored the relation between written knowledge and institutions at least for modern bureaucracies. Like Foucault, Weber attended to the relation of reason and domination: bureaucracies instituted instrumental reason to effectuate their power. But there are important differences between Weber's term *Zweckrationalität* and Foucault's term discourse. Weber's term applies to action and to the forms of consciousness joined to it. Foucault's term applies to language specifically in written texts that have been gathered and formed according to the rules of a social science discipline. Weber's texts are free of any analysis of language; whereas Foucault's are centered on language as a problematic. In fact Weber sees no connection whatever between the social sciences and bureaucracy. Social science is not a historical problem for him. On the contrary, it is a privileged position, in principle separable from the rise and spread of bureaucratic domination. To the end, Weber strove for "objectivity:"

> There is one tenet to which we adhere most firmly in our work, namely, that a social science journal, in our sense, to the extent that it is *scientific* should be a place where those truths are sought, which . . . can claim, *even for a Chinese*, a validity appropriate to an analysis of empirical reality.[24] (*Second emphasis added*)

Weber's Kantian insistence on the distinction between scientific knowledge and social "reality," while perhaps defensible for certain epistemological purposes, obscures the connection between instrumentally rational bureaucracies and social science. In addition it deflects his position away from the analysis of scientific discourse as a configuration of language.

Foucault's position is on the contrary that the effect of scientific discourse on practice may be discerned only if discourse is grasped as a language formation. If discourse is posited either as the work of a subject or as the effect of a non-discursive region of society such as the economy, the operation and effectiveness of discourse is lost. In these cases the register of analysis is shifted to consciousness in the former case or to structured practice in the latter. While these are possible strategies of interpretation they are chosen at the cost of systematically blinding the analysis to the kinds of effects language has when it appears in the form of a written discourse as sanctioned by the institutional framework of a scientific discipline. The intention of Foucault's position is to focus on the internal complexity and external or practical effects of language that is so organized. The statements that are possible to affirm in such discourses, the rules for the formation of these statements, and the system by which such statements are validated in the disciplinary community are the focus of his attention. Discourse analysis is not suited to uncovering the intentions of authors or the determination of discourse in the last instance by the economy. The value of Foucauldean analysis rests with the conviction that the close reading of scientific discourse may uncover language patterns which, when associated with practices, position those practices in definite ways and legitimize the patterns of domination inherent in those practices.

At this point it is necessary to demonstrate the operation of discourse analysis in Foucault's writings and I will do so in relation to his work on prisons. The point to bear in mind in what follows is not so much the validity of this analysis for earlier epochs but (1) that discourse analysis becomes significant for critical theory to the extent that scientific disciplines increasingly are set in place in the social field, (2) that discourse analysis gives interpretive priority to the text, understood as a language formation, over the subject, consciousness, reason and idea, and (3) that particular attention must be given to the need for revision in discourse analysis as the language formations change from printed text to electronic encoding.

Discipline and Punish operates in a relation of opposition to two other interpretive strategies on the history of prisons: the liberal view that the prison is an improvement over earlier forms of punishment and the Marxist view that prisons are shaped by the capitalist mode of production. Foucault rejects both standpoints but he does so differentially. The Marxist position stands in his eyes as a partial view: the analytic of the mode of production permits the historian to make intelligible certain features of the history of prisons, but not those that Foucault finds most compelling.[25] The liberal position, on the contrary, does not serve any analytic purpose; it is rather the object of analysis since liberal principles of the humane treatment and the reform of criminals are the basis of the modern prison system.

The first level of discourse that Foucault must analyze is the Enlightenment reformer's tract, from Beccaria's outcry against the cruelties of the Old Regime system of punishment to Bentham's detailed proposals for the institutional transformation of offenders into utilitarians. The second level of discourse in the account is that of the administrative apparatus: the paperwork required for the operation of prisons and the treatises on the question of controlling agglomerated bodies of human beings. The third level of discourse in the study is that of the science of criminology, the application of systematic knowledge to the administration of the prison. Each of these levels requires somewhat different treatment, but in each case Foucault's interest lies in the way discourse organizes practice into structures of domination ("technologies of power," in his terms). He is not concerned with the degree to which an author's idea is or is not realized in the development of modern prisons. Nor is he concerned with the way social groups mobilize around the issue of the prison to help determine its fate. Foucault's "origin" of prisons is not found in ideas or in actions. The origin of prisons is the complex articulation of a "technology of power" (1) in relation to earlier such formations, and (2) through discontinuous chains of discourses. The "structure" of the prison is set in place in relation to the crisscrossing interplay of the three discursive registers mentioned above.

The prison operates through the production of norms to divide the population into prisoners and non-prisoners. Since the goal of the prison is to return prisoners to the status of non-prisoners, there must be a criterion, one carefully and comprehensively elaborated, to recognize the non-prisoner, the prisoner, and the developmental stages in the change from the one to the other. There must also be a detailed regimen to effectuate the change. There must finally be a method or system of keeping track of the change in each prisoner. Foucault borrows from Bentham the term Panopticon (one who sees all) to denote the entire apparatus of defining the norm, disciplining the negative term, observing the change from the negative to the positive and studying the whole process so that it can be perfected. But there is a difference. For Bentham the Panopticon was an artifice that deflected the criminal's mind from the irrationality of transgression to the rationality of the norm. It imposed social authority on the prisoner in a constant, total manner. The prisoner's actions could be monitored by guards at any time but without his ever knowing it. The prisoner would, in Rousseau's phrase, be forced to be free. With no escape or reprieve from the Panoptical eye, the prisoner would accept the authority of the norm with its rational system of pleasures and pains. For Foucault the task is to see the system as an imposition of a structure of domination, not as a rational, humanist intention.

As we know, the Panopticon, evaluated on the standards of liberal and Benthamite theory, is a failure. Foucault's aim is to grasp the workings of the Panopticon outside the liberal framework: if it does not reform prisoners, what does it do? What are the effects of the social text of the prison, of Panoptical discourse? His argument is that the prison, in the context of a liberal capitalist society that celebrates the anarchy of the marketplace, the chaos of free monads pursuing infinite wants, the rationality of the unhindered subject – the prison in this world imposes the technology of power, the "micropolitics" of the norm. In capitalist society, regulation takes the form of discourses/practices that produce and reproduce the norm. The school, the asylum, the factory, the barracks to greater or lesser degrees and with considerable variation all imitate the Panopticon (see figures overleaf). In modern society power is imposed not by the personal presence and brute force of a caste of nobles as it was in earlier times but by the systematic scribblings in discourses, by the continual monitoring of daily life, adjusting and readjusting *ad infinitum* the norm of individuality. Modern society may be read as a discourse in which nominal freedom of action is canceled by the ubiquitous look of the other. It may be interpreted semiologically as a field of signs in which the metadiscourse of the Panopticon is reimposed everywhere, even in places in which it is not installed. We may suggest that the free individual requires a repressed other, a sort of external super-ego, an absent father if only to guarantee his or her freedom.

In the nineteenth century, the Panopticon suffered technical limitations. It required the physical presence of the observed in a contained, controlled and arranged space as well as the presence of the observer. A guard in a central tower had visual access to all the prisoners' cells which circled the tower and had windows facing toward it. The windows were positioned so that the prisoner could not determine if the guard was watching him or not. The principle of one-way, total surveillance of the subject was extended by the keeping of files. Without a systematic record of the subject's behavior surveillance is incomplete. For the Panoptical machine to have its effect the individual must become a case with a meticulously kept dossier that reflects the history of his deviation from the norm. The emerging science of criminology supplied prison administrations with the impetus and knowledge of record keeping and its evaluation.

In the late twentieth century technical conditions of surveillance have considerably advanced, though Foucault neglected to take notice of them. The population as a whole has long been affixed with numbers and the discipline of the norm has become a second nature. The rough, dirty, illiterate, unruly swarms of nineteenth-century cities, the "dangerous classes," have been replaced in part by a fashion-conscious, intelligent, educated and well-behaved populace.

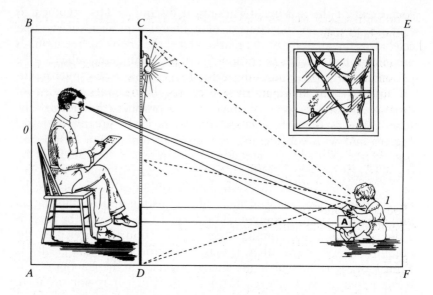

Device for segregative observation in the Guidance Nursery of the Yale Psycho-Clinic. The observers (O) sit in an alcove represented by *ABCD* in the upper diagram and by *A* in the lower diagram. The infant (*I*) is on the floor of the nursery *ABEF*. A 16 mesh wire screen separates *O* from *I*. It functions as a visual sieve permitting one-way vision only. (From Arnold Gesell, *Infancy and Human Growth*, New York: Macmillan, 1928, pp. 32–3.)

Foucault sensed that surveillance in the late twentieth century was something new:

> Our society is one not of spectacle, but of surveillance; under the surface of images, one invests bodies in depth; behind the great abstraction of exchange, there continues the meticulous, concrete training of useful forces; the circuits of communication are the supports of an accumulation and a centralization of knowledge; the play of signs defines the anchorages of power; it is not that the beautiful totality of the individual is amputated, repressed, altered by our social order, it is rather that the individual is carefully fabricated in it, according to a whole technique of forces and bodies.[26]

Foucault notes the new technology but interprets it as a mere extension of nineteenth-century patterns.

Today's "circuits of communication" and the databases they generate constitute a Superpanopticon, a system of surveillance without walls, windows, towers or guards. The quantitative advances in the technologies of surveillance result in a qualitative change in the microphysics of power. Technological change, however, is only part of the process. The populace has been disciplined to surveillance and to participating in the process. Social security cards, drivers' licenses, credit cards, library cards and the like – the individual must apply for them, have them ready at all times, use them continuously. Each transaction is recorded, encoded and added to the databases. Individuals themselves in many cases fill out the forms; they are at once the source of information and the recorder of the information. Home networking constitutes the streamlined culmination of this phenomenon: the consumer, by ordering products through a modem connected to the producer's database, enters data about himself or herself directly into producer's database in the very act of purchase. Marx analyzed the reorganization of labor by capital in the industrial revolution, the massive repositioning of bodies from the fields and ateliers of an earlier age to the factories and later assembly lines of modernity. Similarly one may speak of the reorganization of daily life from the 1920s onward in which individuals are constituted as consumers and as participants in the disciplining and surveillance of themselves as consumers. In this way the spread of consumerist activities from a small élite of aristocrats, down through the bourgeoisie and finally to the masses after 1920,[27] not as an economic change toward a consumer society, nor as a semiological change toward a world of floating signifiers, but as a political change, as part of the reciprocal control of the population by itself.

In addition to an advanced technology (whose capacities were discussed at the outset of this chapter) and a disciplined self-surveillant populace, the Superpanopiticon imposes a new language situation that has unique, disturbing features. The electronic information gathering that constitutes databases, for all its speed, accuracy and computational power, incurs a tremendous *loss* of data, or better, imposes a strong reading on it. Contemporary surveillance in databases relies upon digital as opposed to analog encoding of information. Digital encoding imposes a binary reduction of information. It is a language of zeros and ones combined into great complexities but still deriving from that simple grid. Digital encoding makes no attempt to represent or imitate and this is how it differs from analog encoding. Analog codes are direct imitations of material. Maps are good examples of analog encoding and so are audio tape recordings. In tape recordings minute bits of metal shavings are arranged in an order by an electromagnetic process that imitates the sound waves generated by the music. Thus a high note will produce a configuration of metal shavings that copies the short wave cycles of that frequency. Variations in amplitude are coded as relative depths in the "pile" of oxide particles. Durations of sound are coded as repetitions of the pattern on the tape; the more repetitions the longer the note. If a digital or pulse code modulation recorder is used instead of an analog one the metal shavings are arranged according to a code of zeros and ones. If you examine the configuration of shavings on a digital tape the pattern bears no direct relation to the sound waves.

Just as the letter "k" bears only an arbitrary or conventional relation to the English sound associated with it, so does digital encoding to its material. Written language, however, relies on connotative meanings that are embedded in cultural contexts. Consequently the capacity of writing to "encode" cultural material is infinite, just as analog encoding imitates infinite gradations in its material. Writing accomplishes an infinite expansion of its encoding capacity by the ability of one word to have many meanings. In digital encoding no such capacity exists. In fact digital encoding derives its peculiar strength from the degree to which it restricts meaning and eliminates ambiguity or "noise". If writing in some ways reduces experience and in some ways shapes experience by its internal structure, so digital encoding also imposes its limiting grid and changes its material by doing so. Surveillance by means of digitally encoded information constitutes new subjects by the language employed in databases.

A realist assumption about language underlies the hope that databases will provide "all information in all places at all times." From this standpoint the database is a tool, a technological fix, that perfectly reproduces printed information. This view ignores the productive role of languages in shaping meaning and practice. The thesis repeats the mistaken position that accompanied the introduction of print: that the new technology of language reproduction simply eliminates the errors and deficiencies of the old, that it provides a transparency of knowledge or data reproduction without any loss of meaning or corruption of text. But Gutenberg's invention introduces losses as well as gains in relation to hand-copying. With the introduction of the printing press mistakes and deliberate corruptions were not eliminated but perhaps multiplied.[28] Control over text reproduction shifted from a few scriptoria where small groups of workers could be disciplined and were inspired in their labor by their belief in God (monasteries) or their devotion to truth (universities) to the far more numerous commercial printing houses where profit motives and inclinations to dissident viewpoints easily intervened in the process of reproduction. Similarly the shift from print to electronic means of text reproduction enormously magnifies the possibilities of imperfect reproduction.

The realist assumption, which prides itself on its materialism, also falters by overlooking material aspects of the media. The change from manuscripts to printed texts incurred a loss of the sensuous link between producers and product. The printing machine eliminated or reduced artisanal traces in the product. Designs in the illuminated manuscripts gave way to etchings or even to illustrations. The inefficiencies of lines drawn by human hands were replaced by the repetitive, impersonal pounding of the presses.[29] The book lost a level of signification as a product connected with a specific community of workers. With electronic reproduction, this process advances by several factors. For example, when the Bible is digitally encoded and reproduced through the modem to be incarnated as a file on a floppy disk or as pixels on CRT, the same sequences of alphabetic symbols that graced the pages of parchment have lost a level of meaning by their embodiment in the new medium. Thus Keats's "Ode on a Grecian Urn" in a database of English Romantic poetry is not quite the same entity as the original manuscript, a first edition, or even a textbook for introductory college classes.

I contend that the database imposes a new language on top of those already existing and that it is an impoverished, limited language, one that uses the norm to constitute individuals and define deviants.

A database arranges information in rigidly defined categories or fields. When viewed on a computer monitor or printed out on paper each field is a column and each record is a row. Each field contains a limited number of spaces and if the field is for dates or numbers, entries into it are even more limited in their form. Speed and efficiency of the database varies directly with the fixity of the form in which information appears in it. A database might consist of the following fields: an individual's first and last name, social security number, street address, city, state, zip code, phone number, age, sex, race, unpaid parking violations, x-rated video cassettes rented, subscriptions to communist periodicals. The agency that collects information in this database constitutes individuals according to these parameters.

Many database fields are roughly adequate in relation to the phenomena they signify. As long as the field for last name has enough spaces for characters it does not reduce at all people's names. At the other extreme of fields in databases is "subscriptions to communist periodicals." Here the category itself is politically charged. But the way data is entered into the field illustrates well the discursive function of databases. The name of the journal might be entered into the field but this is less efficient than entering numbers or values for different journals. There might be summary values, for instance 1 to 4, with 4 indicating the most subversive and 1 the least subversive. At this point everything depends on how actual journals receive specific values. *Mother Jones* might be given a 2 and *The New York Review of Books* might be given a 1. In any case, although the relation between journal and value is arbitrary, the number in the field of the database contains no ambiguity. In cases where journals have not been precoded, the value entered in the field is still more arbitrary since it will vary with the person performing the data entry task.

The example indicates that the structure or grammar of the database *creates* relationships among pieces of information that do not exist in those relationships outside of the database. In this sense databases constitute individuals by manipulating relationships between bits of information. But anyone may scribble away or type out this sort of information. What gives databases their effectiveness is not only their non-ambiguous grammatical structure but also their electronic coding and computerized storage. In electronic form data can be sorted and searched with breathtaking rapidity, millions of records a second, practically at the speed of light. In our example above the entire population of the United States can be sorted to search for subscribers to *The New York Review of Books* and this information can be transmitted anywhere in the world in a few seconds. If fingerprints and photographic images of individuals are added as fields in the database, as they are currently in police computers, the power of the database to specify individuals becomes clear.

In *Discipline and Punish* Foucault contends that the methods of discipline that were perfected in the Panopticon were important factors in the birth of modern industrial society:

> If the economic take-off of the West began with the techniques that made possible the accumulation of capital, it might perhaps be said that the methods for administering the accumulation of men made possible a political take-off in relation to the traditional, ritual, costly, violent forms of power, which soon fell into disuse and were superseded by a subtle, calculated technology of subjection.[30]

The change from feudal power to power in representative democracy is a shift from torture to discipline:

> to substitute for a power that is manifested through the brilliance of those who exercise it, a power that insidiously objectifies those on whom it is applied; to form a body of knowledge about these inividuals, rather than to deploy the ostentatious signs of sovereignty. In a word, the disciplines are the ensemble of minute technical inventions that made it possible to increase the useful size of multiplicities by decreasing the inconveniences of the power which, in order to make them useful, must control them.[31]

The discourse/practice of the Panopticon was a condition for a new form of biopower, a means of controlling masses of people for the development of industrial processes.

Similarly, the discourse of databases, the Superpanopticon, is a means of controlling masses in the postmodern, postindustrial mode of information. Foucault taught us to read a new form of power by deciphering discourse/practice formations instead of intentions of a subject or instrumental actions. Such a discourse analysis when applied to the mode of information yields the uncomfortable discovery that the population participates in its own self-constitution as subjects of the normalizing gaze of the Superpanopticon. We see databases not as an invasion of privacy, as a threat to a centered individual, but as the multiplication of the individual, the constitution of an additional self, one that may be acted upon to the detriment of the "real" self without that "real" self ever being aware of what is happening. The figural component of databases consists in such self constitution. The innocuous spread of credit card transactions, today into supermarkets, tomorrow perhaps into classrooms and homes, feeds the databases at ever increasing rates, stuffing ubiquitous computers with a language of surveillance and control. Rather than the motto "all information in all places at all times," an oppositional strategy might better follow Lyotard in his conclusion to *The Postmodern Condition*: "give the public free access to the memory and data banks."[32]

4

Derrida and Electronic Writing

The Subject of the Computer

Whoever fights monsters should see to it that in the process he does not become a monster. And when you look long into an abyss, the abyss also looks into you.

Nietzsche, *Beyond Good and Evil*

Is Deconstruction Computer Ready?

The question I shall raise in this chapter concerns the status of Derrida's concept of writing in relation to the computer: does the introduction of computer writing herald a stage of communication unforeseen and unaccountable by Derrida's method of textual deconstruction, or does deconstruction itself rather open theoretical analysis to computer writing by destabilizing, subverting or complicating writing in a pre-electronic age? This question is not meant to invoke and oppose two technologies of writing: manuscript/printing vs. electronic writing, although the issues I want to raise do have a certain link to the technologies that are a condition for the possibility of various forms of writing. Instead I am interested in the relation between the subject and the text as these terms are reconfigured in the move from print to electronic writing. I am interested in the differences in the way the subject is constituted by the process of writing in the two cases.

More specifically I shall analyze how the introduction of electronic writing functions to destabilize the figure of the subject as it is drawn in the great traditions of Western thought, the Cartesian subject who stands outside the world of objects in a position that enables certain knowledge of an opposing world of objects, or the Kantian subject

who is both outside the world as the origin of knowledge and inside
the world as an empirical object of that knowledge, or the Hegelian
subject who is within the world, transforming him or herself, but
thereby realizing the ultimate purpose of the world's coming into
being. Electronic writing, I shall argue, disperses the subject so that
it no longer functions as a center in the way it did in pre-electronic
writing.

Gregory Ulmer argues that Derrida's interpretive strategy accounts
for these effects of computer mediated writing on the subject. He
contends that "Derrida's texts . . . already reflect an internalization
of the electronic media, thus marking what is really at stake in the
debate surrounding the closure of Western metaphysics."[1] Yet in
order to raise the question of the mode of information Ulmer finds
Derrida's position insufficient. He finds it necessary to carry Derrida's
thought further, developing what he calls "applied grammatology,"
in order "to provide the mode of writing appropriate to the present
age of electronic communications."[2] In the end, Ulmer is unsure if
Derrida already heralds the new age of writing or if he only glimpses
it but does not really come to terms with it. Derrida's relation to
the mode of information contains ambiguities that need to be
clarified.

At several points Derrida explicitly points to electronically mediated
communication as the context of his work. In *Of Grammatology*,
he characterizes the present age as one in "suspense between two
ages of writing," one in which "linear writing" and "the book" are
at an "end."[3] In *Positions* he claims that *Of Grammatology* presented
"the current upheavals in the forms of communication, the new
structures emerging in all formal practices, and also in the domains
of the archive and the treatment of information, that massively and
systematically reduce the role of speech, of phonetic writing, and of
the book."[4] In *États généraux de la philosophie*, a conference of
1979, Derrida's short intervention of 16 pages discussed the role of
"information technologies" on five separate occasions.[5] His main
theme was the need for "vigilance" at a time when the media threaten
to undermine "critical capacities for evaluation" by the "control,
manipulation, diversion or cooptation of discourse."[6] *The Post Card*
too may be interpreted as an essay on the question of electronic or
"tele" writing. Finally, in a 1988 talk at UC Irvine, Derrida pointed
to the destabilization of the subject when the writer uses a computer,
although he did so with his usual strategy of complication. Here
he argued that the computer makes for reversibility and easy
supplementarity of insertion of texts; yet, the computer protects

linear writing by expanding its capacity for integration (that is, the ability to erase annotation, and thus other voices, from the principal text). Thus, Derrida urged, whether the integration is by an author, another person, or a collectivity, the computer destabilizes them, inaugurating a new situation of limits. But then again, he hedged, it may also be understood as extending old situations, old kinds of linear writing.[7] Computer writing then is a minor but not insignificant theme in Derrida's work, a theme, significantly, that is often inserted in his texts at the point at which he is situating his position in relation to the general social context.

In this chapter I shall (1) analyze Derrida's early position on the relation of the subject to writing; (2) discuss several kinds of computer writing in relation to the subject; and (3) assess Derrida's later position, especially in *The Post Card*, as a theoretical strategy for the analysis of computer writing. In the chapter I shall explore both the way deconstruction enables a comprehension of electronic writing and the way computer discourse opens questions about the adequacy of deconstruction, especially with regard to the question of context.

Speech and Phenomena, Of Grammatology, Writing and Difference, Margins, and *Dissemination* argue that certain attributes of writing characterize all experience, that these attributes have been overlooked or repressed in the Western intellectual tradition, and that, in the present situation, the urgent theoretical task is to explore these attributes of writing in order to upset and destabilize the intellectual tradition, because it is limiting or constraining in some way. In order to clarify what he means by writing, Derrida often uses bookish terms even though he is not referring to books in the literal sense. One of these terms is "textuality." In the Western philosophical tradition, thinkers analyzed texts for their "meaning" whether this was construed by logical or rhetorical analysis. The metaphysical assumptions of the tradition define "being," including the being of books, as contained, closed, stable, finite entities which are transparent on the one hand to the author, in the case of texts, and to the actor, in the case of social action, and, on the other hand, to the reader or interpreter of those beings or realities.

In this quest for meaning, certain features of the analytic field are not noticed, even though they are important to that field. Derrida's most common term for this occluded level of reality is "textuality." Dominick LaCapra aptly delineates the term as the "relational networks of 'instituted traces' in general."[8] When Derrida writes that there is nothing "outside the text," he is using the term to refer to qualities of "experience in general,"[9] not just to qualities of books.

These "networks of instituted traces" are differences that make it possible to argue that stable, bounded meanings exist but, at the same time, undermine the claim that these meanings are closed and self-sufficient. Structuralist linguists argue that a speaker cannot competently use a language and at the same time attend to the structure of differences that enable that language to function as a language. Derrida contends that a reader of texts or an interpreter of culture who attempts to uncover stable, closed meanings cannot at the same time elucidate the "textual" conditions under which alone it is possible to have meanings at all.

For example, in printed books words are differentiated by spaces and traces or marks. Also, as contrasted with face-to-face speech, printed books may be distant, temporally and spatially, from their authors. These seemingly innocuous, elementary but fundamental aspects of texts present serious difficulties to those who assume that the world and book consist in knowable entities that are representable in some final way. In this spirit Plato distrusted writing to the extent that he aimed to define truth as a mental experience in which an ideal reality corresponded perfectly to its mental representation, in other words, to the extent that he sought something we call "truth." In its distance from that mental experience, writing is in opposition to speech and is haunted by a certain distance from it. Writing is thus burdened by the "disgrace" of being a mere copy of a mental reality. The theses of the full presence of the word to the mind, of the mind to the real, and of all three to the truth are hallmarks of Western rationalist culture, even though these terms take on very different relations to each other at different points along the trajectory of that tradition.

Derrida's move from speech to writing is an attempt to see writing as always already anterior to speech even as it may "follow" speech in a given situation; it is a method of interpretation that moves from a search for metaphysically fixed meanings to an exploration of the ambivalent play of differences in the "text".[10] His nodal categories – writing, différance, pharmakon – display the concepts of the logocentric tradition as binary oppositions which do not account for this logic. Writing as Derrida uses the term is not in opposition to speech but anterior to the distinction between speech and writing. Speech is always already haunted by the non-identity of author and truth, always already "writing." Since a position which makes a duality out of speech and writing does not take this into account, Derrida develops a different sort of category, a noncategory, one that follows an "undecidable" logic in which an element of "writing" is already within speech, in which the opposition between hierarchical terms is not final or clear, in which writing and speech perpetually "oscillate" so that each cannot be fixed in relation to the other.

As Derrida is fully aware, to argue such a position requires that one submit one's own argument, even in the process of making it, to the 'logic' of difference, to the instabilities of textuality. The seemingly precious or frivolous playing with words in Derrida's writing is but one of his strategies to keep his own writing open to its own qualities of textuality, to prevent its closure and therefore its return to the very position he is attacking. If Derrida were simply to reverse the poles of the binary opposition speech/writing, for instance, to give fixed priority to writing over speech, he would be rendering his own position subject to the very same criticism that he is making of logocentric writers. For that reason he continuously searches for terms that illustrate the qualities of textuality which operate to prevent closure.[11]

The Derridean effort to forestall a closure of meaning in his own text, the insistence on vigilant, unrelenting subversion of textual stabilities, the consistent disruption of logocentric discourse and its attendant subject – these hallmarks of deconstruction have been interpreted by some, including at times Derrida himself, as the first step toward a new politics, a politics that goes beyond the outworn standpoints of liberalism and socialism.[12] The political problem then is the creation, the genesis, the giving birth to the new. Derrida positions his intervention at a transitional point in history: the program of deconstruction appears when the age of the book is over and when the politics associated with that epoch is exhausted.

Such a self-positioning, let it be noted, is not itself new. At least since the Enlightenment, probably since the Renaissance, influential thinkers perceived themselves in an age of transition and saw the need to give outline to a new politics. Closer to Derrida, Nietzsche certainly contextualized his work in this manner. As we shall see in a moment, like Derrida, Nietzsche resorted to the figure of the mother and spoke of the new politics as a "birth." In one joyous mood, he writes, the "free spirit" will give "birth to a dancing star."[13] Alternatively and more ominously, Nietzsche imagined his creation as a terrifying threat.

The question I want to raise concerning the relation of deconstruction to computer writing is about the issue of context and politics. Derrida's contribution to an understanding of computer writing is limited, I shall argue, by the way he figures the inscription of his position in the present situation, and this limitation has political consequences. I accept

1   that deconstruction is a profound critique of logocentric texts and the (male) subject's relation to them, a critique that draws attention to the disruptive role of textuality understood as written traces;
2   that Derrida presents this critique in a situation he rightly defines as one of general confusion amidst massive historical change, inscribing his position as a step necessary to clarify that historical situation;
3   that because logocentrism plays a key role in the present culture its critique has prime political importance;
4   that one major problem is to develop a politics that avoids the totalizing strategies and stabilizing closures of the old "modern" politics, which are closely related to logocentrism.

My differences with deconstruction begin with the way Derrida defines his relation to the present. I am struck by the difference between the meticulous care with which Derrida treats logocentric texts as opposed to the elliptical, vague statements he often uses to define the current situation. His characterizations of the present are general, contradictory, hesitant and unclear about the relation of deconstruction to new forms of writing. It is as if he cannot decide if deconstruction is the philosopher's "gray on gray," depicting the contours of a past age of print writing, or if it is the seer's dancing star announcing the birth of electronic writing. The present situation is an abyss, and looking into it one sees only monsters.

Derrida characterizes, albeit very indirectly, both the new age and, I would argue, deconstruction precisely as "monsters." Derrida situates himself as an expectant mother, but an unusually anxious one. In "Structure, Sign and Play," he distinguishes two kinds of interpretation, one logocentric, the other affirming "play." He urges not a choice between the two but an effort to "conceive of the common ground, and the *différance* of this irreducible difference." This is the position of deconstruction: not to oppose "playful" readings to logocentric readings, but to conceive of the *différance* underlying both. With that in mind Derrida then turns to maternal metaphors:

> Here there is a kind of question, let us still call it historical, whose *conception, formation, gestation,* and *labor* we are only catching a glimpse of today. I employ these words, I admit, with a glance toward

the operations of childbearing – but also with a glance toward those who, in a society from which I do not exclude myself, turn their eyes away when faced by the as yet unnameable which is proclaiming itself and which can do so, as is necessary whenever a birth is in the offing, only under the species of the nonspecies, in the formless, mute, infant, and terrifying form of monstrosity.[14]

Deconstruction is here presented as a kind of giving birth. In the opaque convolutions of the last sentence cited above, Derrida "glances" in two directions: one way toward giving birth to a "conception" etc. of a "question," another way toward those who turn their eyes away from the "unnameable." The former direction appears to be that of deconstruction; the latter that of a new society, a "monstrosity." In the same historical moment, Derrida thus gives birth and the society gives birth. In his giving birth, Derrida does not turn his eyes from society's monstrous birth.

In *Of Grammatology* there is a similar mention of a monstrosity: "The future can only be anticipated in the form of an absolute danger. It is that which breaks absolutely with constituted normality and can only be proclaimed, *presented*, as a sort of monstrosity."[15] Deconstruction, while not named as a monster, may be taken to be that which "proclaims" the monstrous future. After all, in this passage, it is Derrida, the "mother" of deconstruction, who "proclaims" the future as a monster. How then does a mother with such fears prepare for the birth of the new historical epoch? Derrida's preparations are characterized by a double movement: on the one hand, he plays with texts, for some to a point of exasperation; but on the other hand, he is vigilant, obsessively vigilant. At one moment deconstruction jokes and teases with the text; at another, unusual caution, care and seriousness are practised and urged. Derrida recommends vigilant care in the reading of texts with phrases like "patient meditation" and "painstaking investigation"[16] or again "prudent, differentiated, slow, stratified readings."[17] Fastidious preparation is characteristic of the deconstructionist mother faced with "an absolute danger" of bearing a monster in a monstrous age.

In these passages the term "monster" may be read as a sober image of a time threatened by nuclear cataclysm, ecological disaster, totalitarian politics, a post-holocaust epoch in which no nightmare is inconceivable. Or the "monster" may be deconstruction itself, but as seen with trepidation from the outside by those content with logocentric positions. While both of these readings are possible and perhaps even "intended" by the author, the rhetorical/performative force of the image carries a semantic excess, one that spills over the defensive posture toward the outside, one that preempts a bit too quickly the reader's response to deconstruction. It suggests a third reading, perhaps a deconstructive one: Derrida sets into play a binary opposition of the outside, consisting both of society in general and those hostile to deconstruction, and the inside, deconstruction itself. The inside prevents contamination by the outside through the strategy of taking the outside's position and from there designating deconstruction as a monster. But as we know from deconstruction such oppositions do not work the way they are intended: the inside takes on the features of the outside in the textual process of preventing that occurrence. Thus Derrida proclaims that the future is monstrous and that the theoretical strategy that interprets the future, which Derrida is giving birth to, is also monstrous.[18] If my reading has any merit, it might help account for the contrast in deconstruction between fastidious textual analysis and inchoate political gestures.

The politics of deconstruction is connected with and limited by the metaphor of the anxious mother, one who is ambivalent about the future prospects she bears within herself. Some feminists have argued that Derrida approaches texts in a "feminine" manner, not only undermining the male subject that constituted them, but refusing to confront the "opponent" in a "masculine," competitive style.[19] Rather than destroy logocentrism, Derrida, in this reading, prefers to expose its difficulties and limits, allowing them to subsist only now with a more complicated recognition of its partial failure, of its inevitable impasses. Yet Derrida does not take sides with feminism, does not enlist himself to the cause of its attempted cultural revolution. Instead he holds back from this commitment, and I believe he does so in part due to the "maternal" anxiety that the baby will emerge as a "monster." Such hesitation leads to a limited textual politics, one that is proclaimed in the name of opposition to closure and totalization. With the new fancied as both urgently indispensable and ominously forbidding, deconstruction confines itself in a half-way house where interminable labor and playfulness with texts is the main pastime. Deconstruction inserts itself in a field of forces, preferring not to contest the terrain directly but to poke at existing positions, often provoking the opposition's hostile, unconscious impulses.

I have suggested that there may be a problem with the politics of deconstruction for a very specific reason. I argue below that deconstruction is particularly useful in illuminating the relation of the subject to various forms of computer writing and that this capacity of deconstruction provides it with a generality that extends its scope of analysis beyond the limits of its current practice. Like Baudrillard's semiology of commodities and Foucault's discourse on technologies of power, Derrida's textual deconstruction affords access to the complex interplay of electronic writing and new configurations of the subject. However the manner in which Derrida contextualizes his own position may not maximize the ability of deconstruction to explore this relation. And I regard the problem of contextualization as a political question in the specific sense that it determines the field to be opened for analysis.

How then does Derrida characterize the context in which his idea of writing was developed? And what is the relation between the idea of writing and the historical context of Derrida's works?

Text, Context and Electronic Textuality

The politics of deconstruction has often been criticized for its inability to decide one way or another, to take sides, to be with the Left or to adopt some less committed stance. Derrida rightly retorts that deconstruction situates itself at a point of transition between two eras and that the old politics of Left and Right, initiated during the French Revolution of 1789 and derived from the seating arrangement of delegates in a legislative body, no longer applies, or at least no longer serves as a point of orientation to the issues, issues that have yet to be defined.[20] Deconstruction situates itself at an amorphous point that is prior to the formation of a clear politics, prior to any emergence of coherent relations of forces amidst which one may choose sides. The problem of the politics of deconstruction needs to be analyzed in relation to the way it defines its own situation: does deconstruction define itself in relation to the present in such a way that the concept of writing may serve as a point of departure for a critical theory of society?

Derrida is ambiguous about the relation of writing to the present. In crucial passages at the beginning of *Of Grammatology*, he asserts both that writing is part of the "logocentric" past and that writing is beyond this past, inaugurating a new critique of language in the present. While such ambiguity may be unavoidable if the situation is periodized as one of transition, the decisive question is whether Derrida has defined this ambiguity adequately.

Derrida begins by revising the scope of the then current category of language:

for some time now ... one says "language" for action, movement,
thought, reflection, consciousness, unconsciousness, experience, affec-
tivity, etc. Now we tend to say "writing" for all that and more: to
designate not only the physical gestures of literal pictographic or
ideographic inscription, but also the totality of what makes it possible;
and also, beyond the signifying face, the signified face itself. And thus
we say "writing" for all that gives rise to an inscription in general
... the entire field covered by the cybernetic *program* will be the field
of writing.[21]

The category of writing, announcing the "death of the book,"
"covers" electronic messages which are part of the domain of
"inscription in general." But then a subtle shift occurs in the
argument: a distinction is made between "phonetic writing" and
writing of another sort:

> The development of the *practical methods* of information retrieval
> extends the possibilities of the "message" vastly, to the point where
> it is no longer the "written" translation of a language, the transporting
> of a signified which could remain spoken in its integrity. It goes hand
> in hand with an extension of phonography and of all the means of
> conserving the spoken language, of making it function without the
> presence of the speaking subject. ... phonetic writing, the medium
> of the great metaphysical, scientific, technical, and economic adventure
> of the West, is limited in space and time and limits itself even as it is
> in the process of imposing its laws upon the cultural areas that had
> escaped it. But this nonfortuitous conjunction of cybernetics and the
> "human sciences" of writing leads to a more profound reversal.[22]

The onset of electronic information repositions "phonetic writing,"
relativizing it and bounding it, altering the relation of the speaking
subject to the message. The question then is this: does deconstruction
serve as a critique of "phonetic writing" *from the new standpoint*
of electronic writing, or does it aspire only to a critique of phonetic
writing while witnessing from the outside the "more profound
reversal" of electronic writing? On the one hand Derrida includes
under the cover of his concept of writing "inscription in general."
But the "more profound reversal" initiated by the "conjunction of
cybernetics and the human sciences" is asserted after he defined the
field of writing and he makes no attempt to define the nature of the
reversal in question, to define the specific ways in which it alters
writing, or to characterize the nature of the "profundity" of the
reversal. More precisely, does the increased spacing of electronic

writing as compared for example with print initiate a fundamental rupture in the relation of the subject to language and if so how?

Derrida is reluctant to raise this question because, I believe, to do so requires an examination in depth of the context of his own writing, an examination which he calls for but apparently has no desire to carry out. In *Of Grammatology*, for example, he vaguely defines the context of his concept of writing in terms of a certain "situation" of writing that is emerging. He continues: "Why is [the situation] today in the process of making itself known *as such* and *after the fact?*"[23] The question is posed but without further ado is just as quickly dismissed: "This question would call forth an interminable analysis."[24] Since Derrida has already defined his own program as interminable, inexhaustibility is no excuse to bypass the question of context. The program of deconstructing logocentrism finds its opening in the interminableness of the task of contextualization, but interminableness of the question of defining the context of deconstruction is an alibi for a closure of discourse. The only conclusion one can reach is that deconstruction both recognizes its attachment to its context and is unable to define that attachment, rigorously to problematize it and fully to acknowledge the political implications that are linked to that attachment.

In "Signature Event Context," Derrida elucidates the problem of context in relation to his theory of writing, providing a systematic justification for his assertion of the impossibility of specifying the context. He inscribes writing in a problematic of *différance*, as an irreducible absence that resists the identity of meaning and author.

> This is the possibility on which I wish to insist: the possibility of extraction and of citational grafting which belongs to the structure of every mark, spoken or written, and which constitutes every mark as writing even before and outside every horizon of semiolinguistic communication; as writing, that is, as a possibility of functioning cut off, at a certain point, from its "original" meaning and from its belonging to a saturable and constraining context. Every sign . . . can break with every given context, and engender infinitely new contexts in an absolutely nonsaturable fashion. This does not suppose that the mark is valid outside its context, but on the contrary that there are only contexts without any center of absolute anchoring.[25]

All communications, all utterances, all signs contain as their structure, Derrida contends, the possibility of separation from their senders, their speakers, their referents. This postulate is at the heart of deconstruction and is central to its heuristic strength.

But the non-identity of authorial meaning and sign does not justify the subordination or abandonment of the question of context. The theme of "Signature Event Context" is that "a context is never absolutely determinable, or rather . . . its determination is never certain or saturated."[26] This "or rather" is an annoying move, one frequently found in Derrida's prose, because it destabilizes the assertion – in this case, the absolute indeterminacy of context – in a paralyzing fashion. The implication of an incomplete determination of context is very different from that of absolute indeterminacy but neither position is authorized by Derrida as the position of deconstruction. If context is never absolutely determinable there is no point in pursuing it; if context is merely never "saturated" by any particular determination the question still might be worth pursuing and might yield important or at least interesting results. Derrida has not completely excluded the study of context with these assertions. Yet *in practice* his writing too often ignores context so that incomplete "saturation" becomes *de facto* absolute indeterminacy. The contexts of texts by Plato, Rousseau, Husserl, Lévi-Strauss, Heidegger are for Derrida apparently not germane for his analysis of them.

Derrida poses the question of context in relation to the general attributes of the sign. I prefer to raise the issue of context instead in relation to the way an author situates himself/herself in a cultural/social world and even more particularly the way such situating plays a role in determining the author's problematic. I want to claim, in the manner of Sartre in *Critique of Dialectical Reason*, that writers always totalize the contemporary field or context when they select their topic and the manner in which they choose to treat that topic. In relation to deconstruction, I want to argue that its theme of writing is totalized in relation to the context of logocentrism but that it might very fruitfully be totalized in relation to the context of the mode of information, the set of upheavals in the wrapping of language that has occurred in the twentieth century. If deconstruction is specifically set in the context of computer writing, one important subset of the mode of information, a fruitful field of analysis is opened up and, reflexively, deconstruction itself is somewhat reconfigured. By extracting deconstruction from the context of logocentric philosophical and literary texts and reinserting it in the social context of computer writing, deconstruction may better contribute to the work of critical social theory, to its reconstructive task of analyzing late twentieth-century society.

To pursue this problematic I shall first present an analysis of three types of computer writing. Next I shall explore Derrida's text "Envois," from *The Post Card*, indicating the ways in which it opens and fails to open the question of computer writing and the subject. Here I shall return to the issue of the political problem in deconstruction. What is needed first then is an analysis of electronic writing in relation both to the way deconstruction may shed light on its links with the constitution of the subject and the way electronic writing, in turn, is an unexplored context of deconstruction, one that points to its political and theoretical limitations.

Writing at the Border of Subject and Object

Compared to the pen, the typewriter or the printing press, the computer dematerializes the written trace. As inputs are made to the computer through the keyboard, pixels of phosphor are illuminated on the screen, pixels that are formed into letters. Since these letters are no more than representations of ASCII codes contained in Random Access Memory, they are alterable practically at the speed of light. The writer encounters his or her words in a form that is evanescent, instantly transformable, in short, immaterial. By comparison, the inertial trace of ink scratched by hand or pounded by typewriter keys on to a page is difficult to change or erase. Once transformed from a mental image into a graphic representation, words become in a new way a defiant enemy of their author, resisting his or her efforts to reshape or redistribute them. To a considerable degree, writing on a computer avoids the transformation of idea into graph while achieving the same purpose. The writer thus confronts a representation that is similar in its spatial fragility and temporal simultaneity to the contents of the mind or to the spoken word. Writer and writing, subject and object have a similarity that approaches identity, a simulation of identity that subverts the expectation of the Cartesian subject that the world is composed of *res extensa*, beings completely different from the mind.[27] Writers who begin to work with computers report their astonishment at how much easier many aspects of the process of writing have become or that writing is now very much like speaking. The screen-object and the writing-subject merge into an unsettling simulation of unity.

At the phenomenological level of the user's experience, computer writing resembles a borderline event, one where the two sides of the line lose their solidity and stability. Positioned on the line dividing subjectivity and objectivity, computer writing brings a modicum of ambiguity into the clear and distinct world represented in Cartesian dualism. Human being faces machine in a disquieting specular relation: in its immateriality the machine mimics the human being. The mirror effect of the computer doubles the subject of writing; the human being recognizes itself in the uncanny immateriality of the machine. In those instances where the novice user of a word processor discovers the powers of the machine that resemble those of the brain (when moving paragraphs from one position in the text to another, when appending one text to another, when using a spell checker or thesaurus), the mirror effects of this aspect of the mode of information are noticed with shock. It is not simply that new technical feats are possible but that the feats of computer writing appear to equal and in some cases outdistance the achievements and capabilities of the mind. A postCartesian representation of the world might consist in a continuum with simple machines at one end, humans at the other and computers, androids, robots, and cyborgs in between.

When using an electronic thesaurus, the writer instructs the program to search for a string or sequence of letters. The search of the database that ensues is technically unremarkable. But with an unexceptionally fast computer, synonyms will appear on the screen almost instantly after the search command is given. The machine program produced or materialized the word that the computer writer strained to recall but could not: the program achieved an "act of recognition or recall" that resembles successful acts of the brain. The mere thing has accomplished what in this case the human brain could not. Or take the example of rearranging paragraphs: the first time the computer writer accomplishes this task, a sigh of gratitude is involuntarily released. The writer recalls the effort and time it used to take to accomplish this act of editing that now is effortless, consuming barely more time than it takes mentally to rearrange the paragraphs.

To be sure, these examples hardly represent the cutting edge of computer technology; they are small achievements in comparison with the latest developments in artificial intelligence and nonlinear computing. They are not the examples chosen when the computer is seriously matched against the brain as in a Turing test.[28] But debates over the issue of computer intelligence are beside the point. At stake in the theory of the mode of information is not whether the machine is an exact replica of the brain or even superior to it, but whether computer writing puts into question the qualities of subjectivity long associated with writing and more generally with rationality, indeed with masculine forms of identity. The analysis of computer writing as an instance of the mode of information unveils just such an abrupt change.

Advanced computer writers may object that I am pointing to the experience of novices. The thrills of using a computer to write rapidly dissipate as the writer becomes inured to the technology. Computer writing, this objection holds, becomes identical to typewriting or handwriting: the technology, however superior, is just that, a tool and nothing more. Far from unsettling the Cartesian subject, computer writing enables such subjects to compile longer vitae, have more productive careers and generally promotes the institutional patterns of writing that already are in place and that are associated with the autonomous rational subject. While there is much truth to this objection, it overlooks the slow earthquake of the mode of information that is in the process of bringing major changes to the methods of the constitution of subjectivity. One of the signs that such an earthquake is taking place is precisely what may be called the normalization effect. The new forms of subjectivity induced by computer writing quickly become commonplace, taken for granted and denegated. The difference introduced by aspects of the mode of information such as computer writing is repressed and refuted, both negated and denied in the effort to maintain a stable normality. One integrates the new experience thereby living with the changed situation while denying that anything at all has occurred. This normalization or reality effect helps to get one through the day, especially when the day is taking shape so differently from its predecessors.

The interrelation of computerized word processing and authorship changes other aspects of the subject. To the extent that the author is an individual, a unique being who confirms that uniqueness in writing, who establishes individuality through authorship, the computer may disturb his or her sense of unified subjectivity. Unlike the handwritten trace, the computer monitor depersonalizes the text, removes all traces of individuality from writing, de-individualizes the graphic mark.[29] So too does the computer storage media. Compare a novel written on a computer and stored on a floppy disk with one composed in manuscript or even in typescript. Manuscripts have value as originals. Students and scholars consult them in the hope of getting closer to the author's intention, of finding in them the "true" text or of discovering the evolution of the text. The process of composition, of the formation of the text, is materialized in the changes made by the author, changes which are often visible in erasures, substitutions and deletions, in marginalia and additions, in subtle shifts in handwriting, in the entire process of creating a material thing. Large sums are paid by collectors and libraries for such marks of authenticity. One cannot imagine similar interest paid to a file on a floppy disk where traces of originality, authenticity, individuality are precluded.[30]

Computer writing subverts the author as centered subject in yet another way, by introducing new possibilities of collective authorship. There exist numerous methods of collaborative word processing: a disk can be passed or mailed back and forth between authors; two or more computers can communicate on phone lines by use of modems; local area networks provide simultaneous access to a text by more than one computer. In these cases the process of collective authorship, a practice that is common in some disciplines, is facilitated. The computer provides nonsynchronous simultaneity for collective authors: composition and editing can be done in different places at the same time. It also greatly simplifies the entering of additions and deletions to the text. More significantly, the computer-ized writing lends itself to experimentation in new forms of collective authorship.

One such experiment, in which Derrida participated, was carried out in France in 1984–5. Jean-François Lyotard directed an exhibit at the Centre Georges Pompidou entitled "Les Immatériaux," one portion of which consisted in a collective computer writing experiment. Twenty-six writers, from a variety of fields, were asked to compose short comments on 50 words which were selected for their relevance to the exhibit. These "definitions" were stored in a database in a central computer. The writers then had access to the database and could append comments to anyone else's text, with as many as three persons connected simultaneously to the central computer. Writers were asked in particular to comment on "the modifications that this situation brings about in your experience of writing."[31] Lyotard anticipated that, through the use of computers in the composition of texts, language itself might be changed, becoming less oriented toward consensus than toward what he calls "differends" by the multiplication of definitions and their ease of alteration.

Derrida's contributions to *Les Immatériaux* are attentive to the way the technology affects writing. In response to the word "author" Derrida noted that by submitting to the rules of this experiment authorship becomes "indeterminate" and "disappears" as the com-puter technology erases the author's voice and hand. He conjectures

that this postmodern experiment in writing upsets the stability of
the position of the author and leads him and others to search for
"supplementary authority." But he notes also that each intervention
is signed by its author reconfirming older, "modern" copyright laws
so the experiment is not as radical as computer technology permits.[32]
If authors' names were not attached to it, the computer text, with
its multiple definitions of terms, responses to them and responses to
the responses, would constitute itself in anonymity, working, as
Lyotard hoped, to destabilize language, reforming it in an incessantly
provisional play of terms. The new text, I might add, would return
to act upon the writing subjects, dispersing them, releasing them
from the fixity and hierarchy of their positions in the world.

In sum, while computer writing dematerializes the mark, merging
in a new simulation of unity the written object with the writing
subject, it also subverts the individuality of the writer in the marks
it does leave, the files on the floppy disks. Finally, it creates new
possibilities of collective authorship.

Communication and New Subjects

If the "Les Immatériaux" experiment suggests new methods of
composing texts, computer message services offer new ways to carry
on conversations. Computer conversations, I contend, construct a
new configuration of the process of self-constitution. The subject is
changed in computer communications, dispersed in a postmodern
semantic field of time/space, inner/outer, mind/matter. Computer
communications consist in electronic mail, bulletin board messages
and computer conferencing. In these cases, the computer serves both
as writing pad and transmitter: the individual composes a message
on the computer and then, using a modem, sends the message to a
distant point where the messages are collected for future reading or,
less frequently, immediately available to the addressee for response
in a "real time" conversation. The messages may be restricted to a
single addressee, available for any designated number of addressees,
or open to the "public," to anyone who has access to the electronic
"post office." If computer writing substitutes for the printed word,
computer communications substitutes for the postal system, the
telephone, and more radically for face-to-face meetings. The postal
system and the telephone are "tele" communications, sending
messages to a remote addressee. In the former case, the message is
written and communicated asynchronously; in the latter it is

spoken and communicated immediately, requiring a coordinated, synchronous positioning of subjects (or at least a tape recording device at the receiving end). Computer conferencing is a more drastic transformation of the communication situation: participants in the conference remain in distant locations, "attending" the conference only by connecting to it through their computers. Complex, coordinated communications are mediated by the computer, not simply single messages as in the cases of electronic mail. The implication of computer conferencing is that, in principle, human beings no longer need to be in the same place at the same time in order to exchange messages in group situations.

As distinguished from word processing, electronic message services and computer conferencing substitute (computerized) writing for spoken conversations. In this sense they extend the domain of writing to cover areas of communication that previously were limited to face-to-face interactions, mail and the telephone. These forms of computer writing appear to have definite effects on the subject:

1   they introduce new possibilities for playing with identities;
2   they degender communications by removing gender cues;
3   they destabilize existing hierarchies in relationships and re-hierarchize communications according to criteria that were previously irrelevant; and above all
4   they disperse the subject, dislocating it temporally and spatially.

Electronic message services take numerous forms but are normally associated with but distinct from computerized information services. The latter are no more than databases that are accessed through a modem. The user of these services normally pays for access time and is free to explore or "browse" the data to search for desired information. Thousands of such services are available in many different countries, services including everything from library card catalogues to shopping information. Distinct from the information service, the message service provides the user not with fixed information but with contacts to other users. An individual may leave a message for any other user whether or not that user is known. What is so new about message services is that the only identity an individual user has in many of them is a name or "handle," which may be, and most often is expected to be, fictional. The telephone may also be used to contact any number, anyone connected to the network. But conversations with individuals selected by this method are unusual, normally considered intrusive, in bad taste, and practised mostly as pranks by teenagers. By contrast, participants in message services are normally eager to "talk." In addition, phone conversations preserve the signature of the individual in voice and tone so that conversers feel that their "true" identities are being revealed along with their mood. In message services no such traces of identity are preserved. Anonymity is complete. Identity is fictionalized in the structure of the communication.

Conversationalists on message services assume that their partners are not "real" people, even if they are using their actual names, normally considered inappropriate, or if they are expressing themselves as they would in face-to-face conversations. The subject is thus in question in a historically new sense. In the small communities of tribal society, individuals are "known" from birth, enmeshed in extensive kinship structures that reproduce identity in daily experience. In this context the subject is social, constructed and reproduced as a relational self. In cities, by contrast, the individual is extracted from such identity reproduction, but here conversations, before the mode of information, required face-to-face positioning and therefore bodily "signatures" which specified the individual so that, if necessary, actual identities could later be recalled.[33] With writing and print, identity is further removed from communication, but authorship, even under assumed names, serves to fix identity. With computer message services, language use is radically separated from biographical identity. Identity is dispersed in the electronic network of communications and computer storage systems.

For the first time individuals engage in telecommunications with other individuals, often on an enduring basis, without considerations that derive from the presence to the partner of their body, their voice, their sex, many of the markings of their personal history. Conversationalists are in the position of fiction writers who compose themselves as characters in the process of writing, inventing themselves from their feelings, their needs, their ideas, their desires, their social position, their political views, their economic circumstances, their family situation – their entire humanity. The traces of their embeddedness in culture are restricted to the fact that they are competent to write in a particular language, writing perhaps at the infinite degree.

Through the mediation of the computer and the message service, written language is extracted from social communication to a point that identity is imaginary. This imaginary is different from the Lacanian imaginary produced in the mirror stage of development through which all subjects are always decentered and self-alienated.

The computer conversationalist does not reproduce the structural difference between the ego and desire, the gap within the self structured by the unconscious. Instead the written conversation creates the (imaginary) subject in the process of its production without the normal wrapping of context.[34] It may be the case that the subject is always an imaginary one, and that the unified ego is an ideological illusion of bourgeois culture. In computer conversations, however, a kind of zero degree or empty space of the subject is structured into practice: the writing subject presents itself directly as an other.

While the anonymity of the computer message may be experienced by the computer conversationalist as a liberation from social constraint, I am not arguing that such is at all the case. The computer conversationalist is not "free" at all but bounded in many ways: first, to the new, computerized system of positioning subjects in symbolic exchanges; second, by the prior constituting of the self, typically the experience of that self as restricting, evoking the sense of transgression when that self may be concealed or suspended; finally, to the language used in the conversation, with all its semantic, ideological and cultural specificity, a specificity which does not diminish when converted into ASCII codes. I suspect that computer messages may strengthen certain aspects of the subject that were constituted in daily life in a denegated form. I am not claiming that in fact electronic messages enable some "total" or "true" act of self-constitution, but instead that a reconfiguration of the self-constitution process, one with a new set of constraints and possibilities, is in the making.

Message services are commonly found on computerized bulletin boards. Major cities in the United States each have hundreds of them. Bulletin boards are set up by individuals on their phone lines, sometimes in association with a computer club or other special interest group. They are usually free to the caller and offer public domain software files, games and a message service. Messages most often concern questions about computers or about the software available on the bulletin board. Some friendships get started by the exchange of messages and some messages are sent between people who have prior, non-electronic knowledge of each other. One bulletin board in Orange County, California, "the French Connection," is intended to stimulate and simulate a singles bar or dating service. One may participate in private communications with a "lover," "locker room" chats with other men and "powder room" chats with women, or a "public" area where one "meets" other participants.

This message service limits the user to one "handle" thereby reducing one's ability to play with identities. Yet through the handle identities may be shaped that multiple one's everyday self. On the French Connection, a certain "Alice" is remembered for her striptease, accomplished by writing on the screen in the "public area."

Message services are offered by commercial computer information services in the United States and by government communication services in Europe.[35] The most extensive and fascinating experiment in computer communication services for the general public is undoubtedly the French Minitel. Throughout the 1980s the French government, anxious to catch up with other nations in the area of high tech communications, distributed free of charge millions of small computers to phone customers, initially as a substitute for the telephone directory.[36] In addition to phone listings, thousands of services are offered to users of Minitel, primarily databases with current information on a great variety of topics. Although much has been made of the "Minitel Rose" or prostitution contacts,[37] the message service (*messagerie*) is the most popular and most interesting phenomenon on the Minitel.

In Strasbourg, the GRETEL system added a "messagerie" in the early 1980s, a stunning success that quickly spread through the Minitel network. About half of all Minitel calls are for the messagerie.[38] Marie Marchand, in her book about the Minitel, describes some of the reasons for the French fascination with the messagerie: "there are no taboos, one can talk about anything, to whomever one wants, at any hour of the day or night. One can look for a soul mate, pleasantly converse without worry to a total stranger, reconnect with one's regular discussion partner."[39] For the French, "freedom of speech" is most perfectly realized under the conditions of the Minitel messagerie. In 1986 legislation was enacted to regulate "telematic services," like Minitel, under the category of broadcasting media, but special considerations were taken to provide them with the status of the press, ensuring that no programming or censoring laws would apply.[40] In the political arena, the Right attacked the Minitel but the Left cheered its introduction as an extension of the Republican tradition.[41] The Minitel messagerie is thus interpreted as an extension of the liberal politics of communication.

What is striking in these French perspectives on the Minitel is that freedom is now being associated not with the assertion of individual identity in either the public or the private spheres but with complete anonymity. Marc Guillaume, who imagines the Minitel as the basic communications device of the future, rejoices in the protection provided to individuals by the monitor, anonymous individuals who are safely ensconced in a position beyond responsibility.[42] In Marchand's words, "thanks to the pseudo which can be changed at any time, one is able to play a game of masks, of trying on different identities. . . . one is there without being there, one can see without being seen, play at being someone else, venture into the unknown without any risk."[43] The assumption of these writers is that in the mode of information, in the world of the Superpanopticon, surveillance over the individual is complete. The domain of freedom then retreats to the computer monitor and the invented identities that can be communicated through the modem.

This vision is decidedly yuppie: white, male and middle class. A profile of Minitel users that emerged in a 1983 poll confirmed that such is the case: 75 per cent are men; 40 per cent are bachelors between 15 and 40 years of age; most are middle class; 70 per cent of those who use Minitel use the messagerie and 70 per cent of these use pseudonyms because "it gives them pleasure;" 40 per cent assert that they "prefer the Minitel to TV."[44] One may speculate that the Cartesian subject, trapped in a world of instrumental rationality of its own making, has discovered itself imprisoned in a dystopia. Playfulness, spontaneity, imagination and desire all are absent or diminished from the public and private domains of career-building. Only the messagerie, with its fictional self-constitution and perfect anonymity, offers an apparent respite from what has become for many a treadmill of reason.

Connected to the messagerie, one's subjectivity flowers. "Computer cafés," "electronic singles bars," the messageries provide a new form of sociability, a "community" in the era of the mode of information. So attached have people become to their electronic village that, for his August vacation in Brittany, one Parisian would bring only his Minitel. A single woman in Besançon chalked up a record Minitel bill for one month of $11,666, requiring a connect time of 500 of the total of 720 hours for that month. As the success of the messageries mount, as the French telephone service's income dramatically rises and traffic on the Minitel threatens to overwhelm the technology, conflicts emerge between the old and the new social forms. Spouses become jealous over their partners' electronic flirtations; one husband furiously cut the wire to prevent his wife's "affair" over the Minitel (though she was able to splice the wires, upon which he threw the contraption out of the window); another wife left her husband for a "wonderful" man she "chatted" with on the messagerie, admitting to a friend that, when she decided to leave her husband, she had not yet met her new lover. These examples give the impression that the new subjects who emerge in computerized message services are none other than the old romantic individual. What I want to emphasize however is that computer conversations are often considered more important than conventional ones as when some users admit they reveal more intimacies on the Minitel than they do with longtime spouses.[45] Invented subjectivities may be more "authentic" than the "real" self. In the heterosexual examples above, let it be noted, a relationship with "Harry" might prove to be a connection with Hélène.

Electronic Communities

As genderless anonymity undermines the Cartesian subject in the messagerie, so other social hierarchies are put in doubt in computer conferencing. If the Minitel allows private conversations between two individuals, computer conferencing permits any number of people to participate in the same discussion but "at a pace, time and place of their own choosing."[46] If the Minitel provides an electronic supplement for face-to-face interaction, computer conferencing substitutes for the gatherings of entire communities. In Jessie Bernard's imagination, computer conferencing changes "the significance of space for human relationships. . . . we do not need the concept of community at all to understand how a society operates."[47] Other observers are even more sanguine. In their important book on computer conferencing, Hiltz and Turoff cheerfully propose that

> We will become the Network Nation, exchanging vast amounts of both information and social-emotional communications with colleagues, friends, and "strangers" who share similar interests. . . . we will become a "global village" . . . An individual will, literally, be able to work, shop, or be educated by or with persons anywhere in the nation or in the world.[48]

It is doubtful that computer conferencing will alter the world in all the ways and to the extent alleged by its proponents. Still electronic interconnectivity is a new form of writing, interaction and communication, one that further upsets the dominant configuration of the subject/language "interface."

A computer conference is like electronic mail, except that any number of participants (though usually no more than about 50) may be included in the "discussion." Messages are transmitted to a central computer which sorts and stores them, instantaneously making them available for other participants.[49] The order of retrieval is entirely up to the reader, thereby diminishing significantly the role of authorship. To the contrary, the entire conference becomes a single text without an author in the traditional sense of the term.

The process of the discussion is alien and disorienting to those accustomed to synchronous meetings. In ordinary conferences, so much depends not on what is said but on who says it, how they make their intervention, what clothes they wear, their body language, facial and oral expressions. All of this is absent in computer conferencing, as a result of which the subject is placed in a substantially new situation. New conversational protocols to guide the dispersed participants in computer conferences remain to be invented, though some conventions and terms have begun to take shape. "Lurkers," for example, are those who read conference messages but do not contribute to the discussion. And "whispering" means private asides, messages restricted to one or a few of the participants. New "social pathologies" have also emerged. In place of the little fears people experience in face-to-face speech, computer conferencers suffer the anxiety that their messages will elicit no response and in fact participants are in a significant number of cases quite casual about reacting to the communications of others.

Without the normal cues and routines of face-to-face speech to guide the conference, simple procedural issues may raise fundamental difficulties. Problems arise over matters like taking turns and keeping the discussion going. Certain types of statements, those of expository style and logical rigor, tend to stifle discussion, while open-ended statements invite responses and further the work of the conference. Even more importantly, participants continuously must be as explicit as possible about what they are saying, and frequently clarify their statements by the use of metastatements. A good portion of the discussion must be devoted to messages about messages, supplementary information to supply what is ordinarily embedded in the context of speech. Unlike synchronous speech acts, computer conference messages reflect on their own linguistic practice to an unprecedented degree. Because the conventions of speech are so drastically upset, computer conferencing easily becomes talk about talk.[50]

In addition to authorlessness and self-reflexivity, computer conferences upset the power relations, both economic and gendered, that govern synchronous speech. Factors such as institutional status, personal charisma, rhetorical skills, gender, and race – all of which may deeply influence the way an utterance is received – have little effect in computer conferences. Equality of participation is thereby encouraged. New, serendipitous considerations, like typing speed, determine who "speaks" most often. In problem-solving situations at synchronous conferences, pressures are great to conform to existing paradigms or to an emerging consensus. By contrast, computer conferences, with the veil of anonymity and the temporal/spatial distance they provide, encourage open criticism and the presentation of unpopular or eccentric points of view.[51]

Computer conferences also promote the decentralization of power by the simple fact that meetings no longer require expensive and cumbersome spatial synchronization. Advanced telephone technologies, such as communications satellites, permit world-wide participation in conferences. Conference scheduling becomes infinitely more flexible and inclusive. The ideal of participatory democracy of the Greek *agora* and the Colonial New England town meeting becomes technically feasible in advanced industrial society. Hiltz and Turoff foresee the best: "The fundamental effect of computerized conferencing, we believe, will be to produce new kinds of and more numerous social networks than ever before possible. Along with this will come massive shifts in the nature of the values and institutions that characterize the society."[52] In their futurist vision, Hiltz and Turoff are not always attentive to the political process of such institutional change. They assume that the democratic tendencies of this computer technology will be realized by open, free access and wide distribution of skills. Computer conferencing, with its obvious advantages of economy – move words, not people – may become widespread. If so it will introduce a communication form in everyday life that upsets the positioning of subjects in their acts of enunciation.

Writing on a computer, conversing on a messagerie and computer conferencing all introduce new determinations in the author/text relationship.[53] The most seminal change is a new configuration of subjectivity that is constituted not through a textual displacement of logocentric presence but by a form of dispersion of the subject at a level of enunciation different from the author/text relation. The electronic mark, as opposed to the graphic mark, permits a deep reforming of the space/time coordinates of writing and reading throughout everyday life. The electronic mark radicalizes the anti-logocentric tendencies that deconstruction argues are inherent in all writing. The change from graphic to electronic mark permits the wide diffusion of electronic writing throughout the social space and undermines the temporal limits of pre-electronic writing. The chief question then is whether deconstruction[54] offers the interpretive means to grasp the textuality of computer writing, or conversely and reciprocally, if computer writing challenges deconstruction to revise its strategies and move beyond the analysis of logocentric texts.

Deconstruction and Electronic Writing

Derrida comes closest to thematizing electronically mediated writing in his book *The Post Card*, no doubt one of his more elusive works. The first half of the book, entitled *"Envois,"* is purportedly a reproduction of the texts of a series of postcards dated from 1977 to 1979, many of which are missing chunks of prose. The postcards address the question of language as non-communication: "Who is writing? To whom? . . . To what address? . . . I owe it to whatever remains of my honesty to say finally that I do not know."[55] There is no question of attributing the postcards to a particular author, say Derrida (though they might be his and of course the book appears under his name), or ascertaining the addressee(s) (though he/she/they might be actual person(s)), or determining whether the contents of book reproduce, at least in part, actual postcards. Derrida's point appears to be rather that postcards, like writing, are means of not saying in the form of saying. Postcards have the particular attribute of being addressed to someone, being "destined." But they disrupt logocentric reason precisely when they do not reach their destination.[56]

The book jacket reproduces a postcard, much discussed in the text, portraying Socrates seated and writing, while Plato, standing behind him, dictates. This postcard, by inverting the relationship of the two figures, indicates Derrida's theme about writing preceding speech. Plato, the actual writer, precedes Socrates, the speaker so that a possible representation of their relation would reverse the roles, as the postcard does. But postcards, in Derrida's view, are a form of writing and as such play a disruptive role in the logocentric tradition. This particular postcard then may also be said to represent that disruption. As a postcard, it portrays the destabilizing effect of postcard/writing and does so by transposing the Socrates/Plato relation.

Readers of *The Post Card* at first may be confused by the structure of the book. After *Envois*, the section containing the texts of the postcards, there are reprints of two long pieces on Freud ("To Speculate – on 'Freud'" and *"Le facteur de la vérité"*). The relationship between Freud and postcards concerns the similarity of the complex memory traces in the unconscious and the distance effect, the tele-writing of the postcard. In *Civilization and Its Discontents*, Freud regretted the progress of technology and its instrumentalist champions, quipping that while the telephone allows one to speak with distant friends, the same technological revolution made it possible for them to be so far away in the first place, and therefore in need of a telephone.[57] Instead of the telephone, the "technology" that fascinated Freud and that became, according to Derrida, his chief metaphor for the unconscious was the wax tablet or "mystic writing pad." For Derrida, Freud understood that the tablet functioned as a writing tool by preserving traces but also consisted of layers which act differentially upon the writing, preserving and erasing marks in a manner not directly controlled by the writer. Just as the tabletlike unconscious is beyond instrumental reason and therefore similar to the "textual" effect of the postcard, so Freud's fascination with his nephew's game of "fort-da", of throwing the object and retrieving it, remind Derrida of "a certain state of the post ..."[58] In both cases the subject destines an enunciation to an addressee but the message is received by another. In these ways, Derrida finds it appropriate to link his postcards, many of which are love letters, an eminently psychoanalytic theme, with his continuing treatment of Freud.

In *The Post Card* Derrida extends the field of the textuality of writing, with its spacing and marks, to include an account of the medium of postcards. Postcards are sent; they are messages that cover a distance. This "tele" messaging, Derrida maintains, is fundamental to the content of the writing. Writing upsets the rational subject's ability to control the truth because it introduces material traces. These traces come between the thought and the utterance, delaying it, making it different, opening a fissure between the author and the idea. Postcards introduce a further complication. As a consequence of the distance they must travel, they might get misdirected. The intention of the author to send a message to someone in particular might be thwarted, and in principle is always thwarted: "a letter can always – and therefore must – never arrive at its destination ..."[59] Derrida gives much importance to the relatively rare occurrence of the lost postcard because it upsets the instrumentally rational view of postcards as mere tools in the transmission of information. Derrida wants to stress that the off chance of losing the card is inherent in the tele-messaging and cannot be overlooked.

He also stresses other such features of postcards, like the fact that it involves posts or stations, that the information goes from a post to a post. The post is a place of power, he reminds us, not an innocent function. "The 'posts' are always post of power. And power is exercised according to the network of posts,"[60] writes Derrida. As a place of power, the post also changes the message of the postcard, dispersing it in a maze of communicative positions. Post also has a temporal connotation as "after," suggesting deferral and thereby alteration. What is perhaps the most important trait of the postcard is its material configuration: it is an "open" message that anyone who handles it can read, and therefore is communicated not simply to the addressee but to an unpredictable multiplicity of readers. If the writer wants the message to be understood only by the receiver, it consequently must be coded, encrypted for privacy. The postcard is then both public and private. The small size of the space available for the message constrains the writer as well. The message is often just a statement that I am here, some sort of relational message like "How are you?" or "Hello" uttered when encountering someone, not meant to be taken literally but simply a way of reaffirming the relationship. These are the material traits of the postcard that make it a mediating media, that allow it to act like the Freudian unconscious and like writing in general to shape the intentions "behind" words and the meanings within them, to disrupt the control of the message by the sender.

In *The Post Card* Derrida is sensitive to the medium of language, to the way the postcard structures messages, the way it shapes the subject of communication and to the place of the postcard in the history of technology. As Derrida notes, the postcard is hardly the latest development in such technologies. He traces its inception to the Franco–Prussian War of 1870 as a device to enable soldiers to communicate with loved ones back home. But the question of the situation once again evokes ambivalent conclusions from Derrida. In places he suggests that the postcard is a basic principle of writing of an epoch that stretches from Plato to Freud.[61] Elsewhere he suggests that electronic forms of transmission are either different from the postal epoch or a continuation of it.[62] The situation is finally undecidable: are we in the postcard age or is it over; is the postcard an extension of writing or a new form of language; are postmarks different from the marks of electronic mail?

For my purposes, the chief import of *The Post Card* is its presentation of a fragmented and disoriented subject. Derrida shows how writing is a distancing that multiplies and decenters the subject to the point that the reader cannot localize and specify the subject/ author to any degree. "Who are you, my love?" Derride writes in one postcard, "you are so numerous, so divided, all compartmented, even when you are there, entirely present and I speak to you."[63] Neither the receiver of the postcards nor their sender emerges as coherent individuals. They may be specified only vaguely in coordinates of time and space. In "Envois" the postcards are incomplete, with large chunks of texts lost or deleted. The receiver is never clearly named so that she or he could be several persons or one. Ulmer interprets these features of the text to indicate that the author, Derrida, is like the Freudian censor, the position that prevents direct communication.[64] If we compare the postcard to the book, and both of them to the computer, we see a heightening multiplication and dispersal of the subject. In each case the textuality of the writing is quite different.

Derrida is indeed sensitive to differences in the media, differences that concern the crucial issue of the materiality of the trace, but seems reluctant to thematize those differences. He writes: "In everyday language the post, in the strict sense, is distinguished from every other telecommunication (telegraph or telephone, for example, telematics in general) by this characteristic: the transport of the 'document,' of its material support. A rather confused idea, but rather useful for constructing a consensus around the banal notion of post – and we do need one."[65] The last sentence shifts back and forth, hesitant to make an issue of the "material support." Instead of problematizing the cultural configuration of each technology, the interplay of language and situation, the wrapping of enunciation by context, as I am attempting to do, Derride seems to prefer to minimize, at times even to disregard, technological difference in favor of the homogeneity of writing:

> In the years to come . . . it can be thought that it will no longer be writing that will be transported, but the perforated card, microfilm, or magnetic tape . . . the "telepost" . . . in fact these great technologies always really have a metaphysician's näiveté . . . for as long as it is not proven that into each of our so secret, so hermetically sealed letters several senders, that is several addresses have not already infiltrated themselves, the upset will not have been demonstrated.[66]

For Derrida, writing itself already contains the anti-logocentric principle: the difference of new technologies tends to be absorbed within the category of writing. Yet when marks or traces are as evanescent as pixels on the screen, it may be asked if there is anything at all to send, to post, to "destine."

Perhaps more than textuality *per se*, the situation of writing is today being changed. The spacing on the page of the book becomes, with electronic writing, the spacing of the message in the world. With computer writing, spacing is subordinated to a new wrapping of the text: writing could take place anywhere and the electrification of the mark (gramme) calls into question its materiality. With the mark losing its rootedness in space, so its temporality becomes complicated. Computer writing, instantaneously available over the globe, inserts itself in a nonlinear temporality that unsettles the relation to the writing subject. More than books, letters and postcards, computer writing challenges and radicalizes the terms of analysis initiated by the deconstructionist. If traces, spacings and marks destabilize the logocentric subject, what must be said of the textual effects of computer writing, messageries and computer conferencing? In moving from the one case to the other one has shifted from a challenge to epistemological authority of the centered subject to a reconfiguration of identity in a form that puts identity itself radically into question. Computer writing instantiates the play that deconstruction raises only as a corrective, albeit a fundamental one, against the hubris of logocentrism.

The decentering effects of computer writing on the subject are not, of course, entirely unanticipated. The industrial revolution inaugurated transport systems – railroad, automobile, airplane, spaceship – that progressively increase the speed with which bodies move in space. By doing so these technologies may be said to disperse the self in the world.[67] The practice of masked balls, personal ads and clothing styles provide opportunities for playing with identities. But computer writing, as it is being inscribed in our culture, intensifies and radicalizes these earlier forms. To what degree this is achieved will depend upon the extent to which computer writing is disseminated in the future. Only empirical studies of the phenomena can determine their true social and cultural impact. Yet computer writing is the quintessential postmodern linguistic activity. With its dispersal of the subject in nonlinear spatio-temporality, its immateriality, its disruption of stable identity, computer writing institutes a factory of postmodern subjectivity, a machine for constituting non-identical subjects, an inscription of an other of Western culture into its most cherished manifestation. One might call it a monstrosity.

5

Lyotard and Computer Science

The Possibilities of Postmodern Politics

I think being in this room with the computers is more mind work. But the longer you work with it, the more you will trust it. It is hard to learn to trust it. Right now, the men are afraid; they don't trust it, and so there is a lot of stress. They need to learn how to rely on it so they can relax.

A worker in a recently computerized factory, cited by Shoshana Zuboff in *The Age of the Smart Machine*

Computers, Science and the World of Work

The mode of information signifies the end of the proletariat as Marx knew it. As computers are introduced into factories, mediating the relation of worker and machine, a new worker/subject is constituted, one who no longer labors in the sense of the term that was typical of industrial capitalism. Labor is no longer so much a physical act as a mental operation, a cognitive act of interpreting symbols on a monitor. In the words of Shoshana Zuboff, "As the action context is obliterated by new technical arrangements, there is less opportunity for recourse to action-centered skill as a source of immediate knowledge. This means that a return to feelings of certainty, competence, and control will depend more and more upon the quality of intellective skill and the invention of creative methods to tighten the connection between symbol and reality."[1] Artisans and assembly-line workers, whatever their differences, had an active, "hands-on" relation to the materials used in production. Their bodies engaged directly the transformation of raw materials into the finished product. The senses, minds, and muscles of the worker were deployed in a unified effort of mastery and skill. For years on end, the same sights and smells, objects and movements constituted the experience of the worker. Now, since the introduction of computers in the workplace, a new worker is being produced, one who sits, away from the place of production, in front of monitors, switches, lights, an interpreter of information.

And as we bid farewell to the proletariat we must close the books on a whole epoch of politics, the era of the dialectic and the class struggle. from today's vantage point, one can posit the modern period as the age of liberal politics with a socialist opposition. Since the eighteenth century, executive power in Western Europe and North America has been limited by constitutions and representative assemblies. The main challenge to this arrangement came from socialists who argued that qualitative change required the reorganisation of labour. Liberals and socialists agreed that society is devoted to expanded material production: the question was how democratic should be the production process. The introduction of the computer into the workplace and the spread of information systems as the means to control these processes, augurs a new configuration of work and of management, a configuration whose lines are for now indistinct and hotly debated. Some argue that as workers become more skilled, more intellectual, managers must become more flexible, less hierarchical, and that the line between capital and labor is becoming progressively less clear.[2] Others contend that the new workplace is no different from the old, that capital is still in place and that, if anything, workers are becoming more deskilled and managers are becoming more remote from the workshop floor, intensifying not blurring class lines.[3]

Yet one tendency is undeniable: scientific knowledge is increasingly implicated in production. It may be in the form of research and development divisions within the corporation, or in the form of university laboratories[4] connected with corporate projects, or in the form of military initiatives stimulating scientific work, or in the form of market research, public policy research and independent entrepreneurial grants, but systematic knowledge, employing computers and high technology systems, in short, "science," is now the hub of the production process. The problem of production is no longer that of shaping materials, coordinating labor, locating resources, constructing transport systems: it is rather the design, the simulation, the modeling of objects, and later, when they are produced, attaching them to the imaginaries of the consumers. If the discourse of science has become a chief productive force, a discourse that would claim critical status cannot reproduce its moves but must discover a mode of knowing that maintains a certain distance from that form of systematic knowledge pioneered by Isaac Newton and the virtuosi of the late seventeenth century.[5] The procedures of the laboratory[6] and the constitution of the scientist as objective, autonomous, rational, male subject must be destabilized as the basis of knowledge and become its object.[7]

The search for the "other" of science has been explored with some success by feminists[8] and others.[9] At issue is the kind of knowledge one may pursue when the hegemonic modes of knowledge, analytic science and the dialectic, may no longer be taken as foundational. In this chapter I shall evaluate the effort of poststructuralists to recast the question of science on the way to formulating the basis for a new politics. Once the citizen can no longer take up a critical pose as the scientist, as autonomous, rational self in the act of voting, and once the worker can no longer take up a critical pose as dialectical negation, the question arises of the kind of discourse that may properly sustain a critical politics, the kind of self that may act and speak a language of freedom. The question therefore arises of a new politics and of how we are to theorize the political in the mode of information. In order to approach this question I shall trace the trajectory of poststructuralists since events of May 1968 which had great impact on their theorizing about politics.

The Politics of Poststructuralism

Before May 1968 the poststructuralists – Baudrillard, Foucault, Derrida, Lyotard, Deleuze – all had associations or at least sympathies with political groups or parties on the Left. The events of May '68 in Paris provoked a rethinking of earlier political leanings. The student/worker/citizen uprising in Paris and the rest of France did not follow traditional lines of protest and was not led or organized by the extensive network of parties, groups and associations that characterized French politics at the time. The events of May appeared as a sort of cultural upheaval/street theater/happening/performance art as much as a political protest. Wall posters and leaflets put into question not only capitalism, representative democracy, and bureaucracy, but the parties of the Left, the star system of radical intellectuals, and the culture of daily life in advanced industrial society. Conceptual terms from Bataille and Bakhtin are appropriate to describe it. May '68 introduced an eruption of heterogeneity into the politics of modernity, placing in question the accepted routines and assumptions of the Jacobin/Leninist framework. It was a transgressive festival, a display of excessive expenditure, not at all an instrumental, calculating, effective set of political moves, in short, not "modern" politics. With anticipations and reverberations all over the world – Mexico City, New York, Prague, Tokyo – May '68 was a pretext to question the nature and limits of the political.

The political trajectories of the poststructuralists were by no means similar and were not necessarily in harmony with the emerging positions of the 1970s: feminist, anti-racist, ecological, regionalist, anti-nuclear. Poststructuralists, it is true, were in some cases loosely associated with movements for prison reform, gay rights, anti-psychiatry. But they did not take leadership positions within the major directions of protest, clearly align themselves with these movements, or even write extensively on behalf of these causes as had a long tradition of French intellectuals from Voltaire to Sartre for the progressive movements of their day. In fact by the end of the decade strong criticisms by the Left of the politics of the poststructuralists could be heard: Foucault was accused of consorting with the conservative *nouveaux philosophes* and supporting the repugnant neo-medievalism of the Khomeini regime in Iran; Baudrillard, with books like *On Seduction*, was open to the charge of antifeminism; Deleuze's celebration of schizophrenia and nomadism earned him the tag of irresponsible anarchism; Derrida's interminable textual vigilance was denounced as quietist apathy with a new face; and Lyotard, arguably the most politically experienced of the group, was condemned by Habermasians as neofascist.[10] The prospects of a postmodern democratic politics emerging from this group were discouraging indeed.

And yet the poststructuralist meditation on language, particularly as I have contextualized it in relation to the mode of information, does open a path to a new politics, or at least suggests the possibility of such an opening. One's perspective on the politics of poststructuralism greatly depends on how one evaluates the existing political scene. In my view liberal and socialist visions are badly suited to the present conjuncture with its mode of information because they presuppose the autonomous (or in the case of Marxism, collective) rational subject as the basis of popular sovereignty. The world of electronically mediated communication disrupts the interpretive basis of this position. To the extent that the mode of information constitutes a variety of multiple, dispersed, decentered, unstable subjects which contest the culture of identity, a new political terrain may be mapped in which the claims of the "others" of modern politics must be placed in the forefront. The most promising efforts to theorize such a new configuration of the political are Laclau and Mouffe's grafting of the theory of hegemony with deconstruction and Lyotard's philosophy of phrases and differends.

Laclau and Mouffe build on the work of Foucault and Deleuze/ Guattari. In *Discipline and Punish* (1975) and *A Thousand Plateaus* (1980) especially these authors complicate and detotalize the concept of the social in a manner that Laclau and Mouffe adopt and transform. Foucault's "microphysics of power" and Deleuze/ Guattari's "assemblage" are metaphors for the social that deeply contest modern social and political theory. This theory aims to define agents who can have objective knowledge of the social and work to dismantle obstacles that impede their freedom. Politics is here a contest of agents for control of the social and control of the definition of justice. For liberals justice is a procedural matter, a question of the ability of rational individuals to pursue their interests without heteronomous interference; for Marxists justice is ability of united individuals rationally to regulate their affairs. The difference between them, so hotly contested during the past century and a half, is a dispute among white, male humanists, one that in the long run may turn out to inscribe a difference no greater than and analogous to that between Catholics and Protestants, both of whom after all are Christians.

Foucault disputes the definition of the political in modern social theory by multiplying and desubjectivizing the political field. He argues that, in "modern" politics, the law is the center of power, a function which variously impedes or promotes the action of individuals. In a typical poststructuralist move, Foucault looks to the margins for evidence to destabilize this inscription. He finds power at play in all practices, not only in those that directly contest the central legal authority. Power is at work among doctors who determine the sexual identity of hermaphrodites, for example.[11] For Foucault, power is dispersed throughout human relations. The deception of modern politics is the pretense to confine the locus of power to the central government, filtering from awareness its multiple, ubiquitous forms. If power is in effect everywhere, it may legitimately be contested not only at the center but also at the margins. One important effect of the dominant discourse is to secrete these diffuse subversions, allowing only certain agents to appear on the scene as "political." Foucault's critique of modern politics resonates with the eruption of protest movements in the 1970s, which often occurred outside the established arena of liberal and social disputes.

Foucault also recasts the position of the subject in politics. Modern politics is grounded in a Cartesian view of the subject as a rational being who is "outside" the world of objects and who may control them by knowing them. Foucault refutes this view by unsettling the dualism of subject/object, knowing/doing, idea/action, discourse/ practice. He "objectivizes" the social by locating the play of power in configurations of discourse *and* practice, configurations that are in the end neither subjective nor objective. The prison constitutes a "technology of power" through a complex of architectural design, administrative rules, scientific knowledge and legal apparatuses. Its power cannot be located in any subject so there is no agent to rebel against. Foucault contests the liberal celebration of the modern prison as a humane advance over earlier barbarisms by deflecting attention from the issue of the reform of prisoners to the mechanism of administrative power, the Panopticon, a form of domination obscured by liberal discourse. His analysis points not to the modern question of the transformation of criminals into rational subjects, but to the issue of how subjects are constituted through the operations of a particular discourse/practice. The implication is that even "rational" subjects are so constituted.

A postmodern politics, for Foucault, implies the eruption of the heteronomous, the push of the transgressive gesture at the margins of the social that reveals the play of power where before it had been hidden, the displacement of established discourse by "local knowledges." In this case the figure of the autonomous subject is necessarily relativized and along with it the position of the theorist is put into question. For the theorist is implicated in the critique of agency: if the model of the rational subject is invalidated in Foucault's critique of centered power, the position of theory is also called into question. The theorist has no more right to stand on the solid ground of rationality than has the social agent. To that end Foucault disputes the universal claims of the intellectual in the Western tradition and the totalizing claims of its theorists from Locke to Marx. But the status of Foucault's own theory and its claim to critical status are thereby also in doubt.

Habermas for one strongly objects to what he calls "the performative contradiction" in Foucault's Nietzschean discourse, in which no single perspective can serve as a ground of truth.[12] In defense, Foucault denies adherence to "irrationalism" by returning to one aspect of Enlightenment thought: its "spirit of critique."[13] The problem, as Foucault sees it, is to authorize space for a critical discourse when the object in question is the tradition of critical discourse itself. A position of critique is possible, he contends, which invokes norms without grounding them, which pursues "truth" without constituting the subject as centered in truth. Regardless of the adequacy of this response, Habermas's complaint of performative contradiction, that by instantiating the critique of reason one necessarily at the same time invokes the rules of reason, presumes a unified, homogeneous textual field that allows no "contradiction" in the first place. But if discourse is always already heteronomous, complicated by absences and impasses, as poststructuralists maintain, this charge loses much of its force.

Postmodern Desire

In *A Thousand Plateaus* Deleuze and Guattari articulate in somewhat greater complexity than Foucault a vision of the social as decentered and desubjectivized. Their earlier work, *Anti-Oedipus*, relies upon a suspect notion of schizophrenic desire to criticize Freudian and Marxist views. *A Thousand Plateaus* continues to present a problematic view of desire as a ground of critique, but contains promising elaborations of a postmodern theory of the social and political. The book attempts to disrupt a linear presentation of theory: "The two of us wrote *Anti-Oedipus* together. Since each of us was several, there was already quite a crowd. . . . A book has neither object nor subject; it is made of variously formed matters . . . To attribute the book to a subject is to overlook this working of matters, and the exteriority of their relations."[14] Without a centered subject directing the reader from one step to the next, *A Thousand Plateaus* challenged modern theory in its textual form. In the same vein, Deleuze and Guattari encourage readers to begin anywhere since the book is not organized as a continuous, linear discourse.

Deleuze and Guattari configure the social as a complex of bodily intensities in a state of continuous nonlinear movement. The logic they present is multidimensional, shifting, discontinuous. They speak of strata, assemblages, territorializations, lines of flight, abstract machines, a congerie of terms that disrupts the function of concepts to control a field through discursive articulation. Their categories cut through the normal lines of comprehension, the binary logic that governs modern social theory to present a picture of reality from the perspective of a sort of primitive life force. It is as if the earth itself were to describe the changes on its surface in the course of human history, a vantage point quite remote from the ego of the individual or from the disciplined consciousness of the social scientist.

Of particular interest to the development of a postmodern politics is the way Deleuze and Guattari configure the present in terms of language and action. They write,

> capitalist organization in its entirety, operates less and less by the striation of space–time corresponding to the physicosocial concept of work ... [and more and more by] a generalized 'machinic enslavement,' such that one may furnish surplus-value without doing any work (children, the retired, the unemployed, television viewers, etc.) ... capitalism [now] operates less on a quantity of labor than by a complex qualitative process bringing into play modes of transportation, urban models, the media, the entertainment industries, ways of perceiving and feeling – every semiotic system.[15]

In this vision of the postmodern world individuals are constituted through their place in the circuit of information flows. Staying tuned in is the chief political act.

In the late twentieth century a new "assemblage" is formed within capitalism that "reterritorializes" the relation of human and machine:

> If motorized machines constituted the second age of the technical machine, cybernetic and informational machines form a third age that reconstructs a generalized regime of subjection: recurrent and reversible "humans-machines systems" replace the old nonrecurrent and nonreversible relations of subjection between the two elements; the relation between human and machine is based on internal, mutual communication, and no longer on usage or action. ... with automation comes ... a new kind of enslavement ... one is enslaved by TV as a human machine insofar as the television viewers are no longer consumers or users, nor even subjects who supposedly "make" it, but intrinsic component pieces, "input" and "output" feedback or recurrences that are no longer connected to the machine in such a way as to produce or use it. In machinic enslavement, there is nothing but transformations and exchanges of information ...[16]

The opposition of subject and object cannot serve to make sense of these new dispositions of humans and machines. A new vision is required to comprehend the master/slave relation in the form of circuits.

A Thousand Plateaus advances our understanding of the political by its nonlinear presentation of just such a social world but it grounds its analysis on a suspect notion of freedom as the flux of desire. Against the schizoid pullulations of the unconscious, the human/computer interface becomes an "enslavement." But the authority for this judgment proceeds from the privilege accorded to desire in the first place. Deleuze and Guattari retreat to the position of theorist/legislator proclaiming the truth of desire against the degradation of "the machinic assemblage," a retreat that returns them to the modern position which they sought at the outset to undermine. The hermeneutic of desire closes their work against its claims of multiple, non-centered authorship. They become once again the "subject" that promotes the cause of desire, a unitary subject whose illocutionary force constrains the reader even in the book's anti-authoritarian organization.

Toward PostMarxism via Deconstruction

Without Deleuze and Guattari's metaphysics of desire, Laclau and Mouffe posit a decentered, differential view of the social. They turn to poststructuralism because it offers the basis for a non-identitarian critical theory. Marxism, as well as liberalism, on the contrary, impose a theoretical discourse that closes and centers the social by resort to a self-identical subject. In *Hegemony and Socialist Strategy* Laclau and Mouffe want to defend the thesis "of continuity between the Jacobin and Marxist political imaginary which has to be put into question by the project for a radical democracy." Such discourses are "constituted as an attempt to dominate the field of discursivity, to arrest the flow of differences, to construct a center."[17] Laclau and Mouffe offer a concept of "articulation" that remedies these deficits:

> if we accept the non-complete character of all discursive fixation and, at the same time, affirm the relational character of every identity, the ambiguous character of the signifier, its non-fixation to any signified, can only exist insofar as there is a proliferation of signifies. . . . Society never manages to be identical to itself, as every nodal point is constituted within an intertextuality that overflows it.[18]

Critical theory for them must be poststructuralist because society is non-identical. By maintaining linguistic instability at the theoretical level, the social for them becomes intelligible in a way that is appropriate to a democratic politics. The "centering" tendency in liberal/Marxist discourse, they claim, works against the democratic tendency in politics.

They illustrate this argument by redefining capitalism. The capitalist order is, for Laclau and Mouffe, necessarily unstable, characterized by continuous "antagonisms." Hegemony is achieved by the denial of this instability, by the discursive construction of the social as fixed, natural, inevitable. Yet language intrudes a relational logic of differences that subverts hegemonic discourse, maintaining always the possibility of new connections, of new statements by which the other imposes antagonistic recognition on the self. Laclau and Mouffe offer a politics of pluralism that would accept the condition of difference and antagonism as a basis for a new democracy. In their words,

> Pluralism is *radical* only to the extent that each term of this plurality of identities finds within itself the principle of its own validity, without this having to be sought in a transcendent or underlying positive ground for the hierarchy of meaning of them all and the source and guarantee of their legitimacy. And this radical pluralism is democratic to the extent that the autoconstitutivity of each one of its terms is the result of displacements of the egalitarian imaginary.[19]

Capitalism is open to criticism because it impedes the process of reconfiguration of identity, the instability that defines postmodern democracy. The theoretical argument for such a pluralism is developed, as we shall see below, most cogently in the work of Jean-François Lyotard.

Laclau and Mouffe boldly posit a "postMarxist" political theory by introducing poststructuralist themes into a revised Gramscian theory of hegemony. They attempt to outline a non-essentialist social theory in which objectivities are never seen as self-identical, in which history is not theorized as a closed chain of necessarily unfolding events. The notion of hegemony signals, for them, the necessary incompleteness of any Marxist theory. The concept of hegemony was introduced by Gramsci and others as a supplement to account for social phenomena such as class consciousness that were not accounted for by the closed logic of forces and relations of production. For Laclau and Mouffe the issue is not that Marxism may need newer and better supplements (Freud, Sartre, etc.) but that supplementarity is a necessary component of all theory. Theory for them must incorporate "incompleteness" to avoid essentialism and the illusion of controlling the social.[20] The supplement both completes the theory and reasserts its necessary incompleteness.

Laclau and Mouffe attempt to configure the social in a non-essentialist manner as follows. Worldly positivities are a confluence of "articulations" and "antagonisms." Daily life is a composite set of particularizations of relations of force which conceal their origin and their relativity by suppressing what is outside them. Identities are achieved by occluding differences. Laclau cites Saint-Just to the effect that "The unity of the Republic is only the destruction of what opposes it."[21] Society is thus composed of positions that are relational but which systematically deny their relationality. The social fabric invites a deconstructive analysis which destabilizes identities by "reading" their suppressed absences back into them. Laclau and Mouffe argue for theoretical undecidability, for incompleteness and contingency as strategies for representing the play of antagonisms in history.

The textuality of the social is evident in the practice of naming. In *Capital* Marx spoke of the hieroglyph of the commodity as if it were an exceptional duplicity of the capitalist mode of production. Laclau and Mouffe insist on the inevitability of names and the deconstructive logic it bears within itself, on a generalized hieroglyphic logic. History for them may be figured as a double process by which forces both inscribe and empty their names with signifiers. The signifier "liberalism" is defined by inclusions and exclusions at different times and in different places. As a signifier, liberalism is ideologically most effective in simulating consensus, in unifying its referential objects, when it is empty. When the signifier is highly ambiguous and unstable is ironically the moment when it is most transparent to the agents who bear its identity. Radical democracy is furthered, Laclau and Mouffe contend, when identities are negotiated in contingency and incompleteness.

One problem with their position must be noted. A certain mirroring of theory and society insinuates itself in their discourse: a deconstructive theory reveals a deconstructable social world. They criticize Foucault's distinction between discursive and nondiscursive practices, for instance, by arguing that non-discursive practices are at bottom discursive; "if the so-called non-discursive complexes – institutions, techniques, productive organization, and so on – are analyzed, we will only find more or less complex forms of differential positions among objects . . . which can only . . . be conceived as discursive articulations."[22] Foucault cannot posit a nondiscursive realm, Laclau and Mouffe contend, because the social becomes meaningful only through its appearance in discourse as differential relations. Nothing then is beyond the text, more specifically the deconstructive text. If that is so, closure has been reintroduced in Laclau and Mouffe's position. They have repressed the non-discursive in order to render the field of the social totally amenable to deconstructive tactics. Deconstructive society is purchased at the cost of totalizing the intellectual strategy of deconstructive textuality. Postmodernism thereby recedes to the modernist theoretical impulse to "suture" or control its object. Foucault's position, maintaining a place for the nondiscursive even if only as a horizon of non-intelligibility, has, I would claim, the advantage of curtailing the impulse to totalization.

Laclau and Mouffe seek to protect themselves from this surreptitious reintroduction of essentialism by noting the political trend toward a contestation of hegemonic identities in the new social movements. They assert that the current "terrain" is no longer suitable for Marxist critique, without delineating adequately the features of the current situation that authorize this judgment. Their intervention reads as a *philosophical* critique in the sense that poststructuralist concepts replace Marxist ones because of the greater power of the former to render intelligible the field of the social. In debates with Marxists, who invoke the revolutionary potential of the proletariat and the force of the capitalist mode of production, Laclau and Mouffe are able to challenge their opponents' positions more on theoretical than on contextual grounds.[23]

I argue that another step must be taken to disrupt the tendency of their theory to present itself as universally true. The mode of information, as I have presented it, introduces a contextual contingency in the strategy of deconstructive hegemony. In other words, through the inscription of electronically mediated communication, the social world is textualized in a form that lends itself to poststructuralist strategies of reading. The context of the mode of information gives generalizing force to these strategies and introduces into them a dose of historicizing contingency. Hence their truth claims are both general and particular, neither "universal" nor "relative." And hence the theorist, Laclau and Mouffe, is not inserted in the discourse as a fixed, transcendental signifier.

Lyotard on Postmodernity

With Foucault, Deleuze/Guattari and Laclau/Mouffe the tendency toward a postmodern political theory concerns the multiplication of the sites of power and resistance, as well as an effort to complicate the social, to extricate it from the theoretical clutches of analytic and dialectical reason, to redefine it as a locus of contingency, absence and linguistic uncertainty. These same directions are taken in the recent work of Jean-François Lyotard who most explicitly addresses the question of the political as the problem of postmodernity. *The Postmodern Condition* (1979) and *The Differend* (1983) may be interpreted as rigorous efforts to open a new terrain of politics. Like the other poststructuralists I discuss in earlier chapters, Lyotard defines his theme in terms of language, in particular the discourse of science. More than the other theorists, however, Lyotard explicitly draws connections between language and electronic mediations, on the one hand, and the contemporary social context, on the other hand. In this sense, Lyotard, especially in *The Postmodern Condition*, closely approaches the problematic of the mode of information as I have defined it in this study.

In the opening sentence of *The Postmodern Condition*, Lyotard sharply presents the issue: "The object of this study is the condition of knowledge in the most highly developed societies."[24] Lyotard considers "knowledge" to be science, especially natural science, registering the tremendous importance of this body of discourse in all dimensions of contemporary affairs and institutions. Science is today not simply a set of disciplines, segregated in various departments in institutions of higher education but a force that provides fundamental knowledge in the economy, the military, and the state. Even the disciplines of the social sciences measure their legitimacy, the status of their endeavors, by the degree to which their methods approach those of "the hard sciences." We are in the age of "big science," as Laurie Anderson sings. Scientists themselves are too modest when they propose that their work is bounded by the methodological routines of the laboratory, the professional conference and specialized journals, strongly demarcating what they do from the epistemologically "lesser" activities of technical application. Decades ago Galbraith, in *The New Industrial State*, acknowledged the rising social significance of science by designating "the scientific estate," going so far as to suggest this class as a new ruling class.[25] With disingenuous humility, scientists for the most part are content to enjoy their high status, receive huge federal grants and flatly abrogate social responsibility.

Lyotard attends to two features of contemporary science: its legitimating protocols and its relation to the computer. Through an analysis of these themes he lays the basis for his argument of postmodernity: that a new era of politics is emerging, one that brings to a close two centuries of Jacobinism and Leninism, two centuries of modernity. *The Postmodern Condition* is as sweeping in its claims as it is polemical in tone. It broadly challenges the reader to awaken from complacent modernist slumbers and consider the possibility that fundamental transformations are occurring unannounced, surreptitiously but occurring nonetheless, and doing so with ever greater frequency. The later work, *The Differend*, develops perhaps more rigorously the philosphical basis for some of the claims made in 1979. It also retreats from some of the earlier positions, preferring a less global, less sociological approach. At this point, I shall examine Lyotard's critique of science regarding first the problem of legitimation and second the issue of computerization.

The basis of Lyotard's analysis in *The Postmodern Condition* is a judgment that an extreme situation exists, that there is a "crisis of narratives," that the grand perspectives of an earlier epoch are no longer believable. One may easily deny this judgment for it is impossible to verify or to substantiate it to a skeptic's satisfaction. Yet if it is accepted the important claims of Lyotard's position become urgent: that we are perhaps in a new "postmodern" situation with qualitatively new possibilities and challenges. He makes every effort to substantiate his judgment of crisis but he is aware that his discourse is a "strategy" (p. 7), the taking of a position which is bound to provoke controversy and even invites critique and refutation. Lyotard draws evidence in support of his claim of a crisis from several intellectual domains. His most telling arguments, however, concern science itself.

Taking what we have seen to be a typically poststructuralist turn, Lyotard argues that the decisive level of social analysis in the postmodern age is language. This is so for the historical reason that the rise of the media gives a new prominence to language (p. 16) and for the logical reason that "language games are the minimum relation required for society to exist" (p. 15). An analysis of this linguistic component of contemporary society reveals, for Lyotard, the outlines of a fundamentally new situation: an opening toward a culture of multiplicity through a collapse of the totalizing or unifying discourses of narrative and science.

Lyotard's distinction between narrative and science has striking similarities with that of myth and enlightenment in Adorno and Horkheimer's *Dialectic of Enlightenment*. In both cases the premodern and the modern are distinguished and compared at a discursive level. Written in the dark mood of the time of Auschwitz in 1944, *Dialectic of Enlightenment* denounces the then current interpenetration or synthesis of myth and enlightenment in fascism and mass culture. Enlightenment domination of nature changes dialectically into a nightmare of the domination of man, with little hope for a rosier turn of the dialectic in the future.[26] In *The Postmodern Condition* the relation of science to narrative is more complex: science requires narrative for its legitimating function: "Scientific knowledge cannot know and make known that it is the true knowledge without resorting to the other, narrative, kind of knowledge, which from its point of view is no knowledge at all" (p. 29). In recent years these metanarratives of science, such as the story of progress, have lost their coherence. At stake in this crisis, for Lyotard, is the emergence of a new science, a postmodern science based on new narrative types.

Lyotard distinguishes science from narrative as types of discourse which have different "pragmatics" of language, or language games. In traditional narratives, any member of society may occupy the post of speaker. The positions of speaker, listener and referent of the narrative are fluid and individuals in turn take on each of them. In these face-to-face encounters, society is reproduced through the iteration of the narrative in a way that does not require a separate discourse to legitimize the narrative and that creates a cyclical temporality by denying any difference in the repetition of the story from earlier instances. By contrast, scientific knowledge has a different logic: it permits but a single language game, that of denotation; it creates a relation of mutual exteriority with respect to society; it requires competence only of the scientist or the speaker, not the listener; it gives no special value to the act of reporting its findings; and its discursive temporality is linear, not circular.

Although science is critical of narrative discourse, in one particular sense it relies upon narrative: that is, science relies on narrative for legitimation. From Plato onward, Lyotard contends, science sought a ground in narrative, in a form of discourse itself not scientific. Until recently, this relation was reproduced as the task of philosophy. The discipline of philosophy justified itself in part as the leading discourse by its role as provider of the ground of science. In *The Postmodern Condition* Lyotard distinguishes two philosophical narratives that furnished science with a ground: the idea of progress (p. 31) in Britain, France and the United States, and the idea of education as promoting the health of the nation (p. 34) in Germany. Lyotard's aim, however, is not to rehearse the history of science in relation to narrative but to point out that these narratives of science are no longer credible. What becomes of science, and the society which so deeply relies upon it, Lyotard asks, when its project is delegitimized? And my question, the one central to this study, may be added to his: what happens when electronic means of generating and disseminating science become available and are practised?[27]

Lyotard conceives science today in the postmodern condition of multiple language games: "science plays its own game; it is incapable of legitimating the other language games" (p. 40). Without its own legitimizing narrative, science retreats within itself, a situation that opens up the discursive field to the proliferation of "new languages," none of which are legitimized by a grand narrative and none of which requires being so legitimized: "This is what the postmodern world is all about. Most people have lost the nostalgia for the lost narrative. It in no way follows that they are reduced to barbarity. What saves them from it is their knowledge that legitimation can only spring from their own linguistic practice and communication interaction" (p. 41). In his own way, Lyotard thereby legitimizes the condition of nonlegitimation, the postmodern condition of infinitely proliferating language games.

Lyotard draws attention to two tendencies concerning the status of legitimation in science under the postmodern condition, each of which appears to militate in different, conflicting directions. First, some sciences develop self-justifications and images of nature which confirm the postmodern condition. Second, science expands its relation to society, its relation to the performativity, or the instrumentality of society. Computerization aids in both of these opposing tendencies.

Lyotard is fascinated by the theoretical implications of certain new tendencies in scientific research, mostly in physics. At least since Werner Heisenberg's indeterminacy thesis the metanarrative of science as the progress of objective truth has been placed in question. The scientist *qua* subject could no longer be regarded as epistemologically distinct from the object being studied. The knowledge generated by scientific experiment took on the status of yet another language game, a form of truth confirmed by the community of the speakers in that game, not in any sense an objective, universal truth. Lyotard cites recent developments within science that further destabilize the metanarratives of science, especially those of a positivist kind. Mandelbrot's fractals and René Thom's catastrophe theory are "changing the meaning of the word *knowledge*, while expressing how such a change can take place. [They are] producing not the known, but the unknown" (p. 60). This postmodern science produces a new narrative of legitimation, "the little narrative" of "paralogy," the scientific work that calls attention not to its denotative statements but to its requirement for rules, "prescriptive utterances" that are necessary for science but that are not themselves science.

Surprisingly and unfortunately, Lyotard fails to mention in this context the feminist critique of science which also calls into question the purely denotative status of science as well as the validity of its metanarratives. Keller and others have shown the connection of science with the subject/object dualism that founds knowledge as the control of nature.[28] They convincingly connect the figure of the scientist as knower with masculine forms of subjectivity, calling for new patterns of subject/object relations within science. The feminist proposal to invent a new science with a new, nondominating relation to nature is in fundamental agreement with Lyotard's perspective on postmodern science as multiple narratives and ought to form a part of his critique. Lamentably Lyotard, like the other theorists discussed in this volume, does not adequately come to terms with the writings and perspectives of feminism either in general or in relation to particular topics being treated.

The chief connection between Lyotard's investigation of postmodern science and my work on the mode of information concerns the question of the computerization of science and the role it plays in the development of postmodern science. Throughout *The Postmodern Condition* Lyotard is sensitive to the increasing role of computers in society in general; indeed, this is one of the leading themes of the book. He is, however, very ambivalent about this role, at times configuring the computer as the culmination of modern metanarratives and social practices, at other times crediting computerization with promoting postmodernism. For example, Lyotard discusses the relation of modern science to society, indicating how science confirms bourgeois social relations, depends on those forms, all the while negating those relations in its claims of autonomy. Computers play an important role, according to him, in this context: like prosthetic devices, they extend the performativity of the system (p. 44). But computer technology, Lyotard reminds us in the spirit of Heidegger, only comes into play in a general social context in which performativity is already the master code. Computers heighten "context control," the Orwellian elimination of contingency by the powers that be:

> it is precisely this kind of context control that a generalized computerization of society may bring about. The performativity of an utterance, be it denotative or prescriptive, increases proportionally to the amount

of information about its referent one has at one's disposal. Thus the growth of power, and its self-legitimation, are now taking the route of data storage and accessibility, and the operativity of information. (p. 47)

For Lyotard modern science, armed with computers, presents a dangerous threat to freedom.

The theory of computerization – cybernetics – provides a model for system control that equates contingency with noise, with loss of information. The social ideal of cybernetics is the elimination of contingency and the maximization of control by the system. Computers then play a double role, Lyotard contends, in promoting the efficiency principle of modern society: as theory and as machinic practice. In neither case does he analyze systematically or in great detail the relation of computerization to science. Instead he makes suggestions in passing about the important role computerization has for science, without specifying the nature of this role. As a thematic essay on the state of knowledge, *The Postmodern Condition* cannot perhaps be expected to do any more. Yet the question of computerization and science is raised and it is tempting to consider the issue in more depth. Lyotard has stated that cybernetics is a new language game, one that is of great importance to science. We may ask, exactly how important is it? Which discursive domains within science does cybernetics regulate? And how important are these to the overall fate of science in contemporary society? What is the relation between cybernetic theory and the use of computers by scientists? Does the success of the theory affect the spread of the technology? Or is the reverse true? What is the effect of the technology on the theory?

Computer Science and Postmodernism

To pursue the question of the relation of computers to science, I did a brief study of the discipline of Computer Science. I examined texts which speak to the issue of the definition of Computer Science. Specifically I looked at the Turing Award papers of the past two decades which appeared in the *Association for Computing Machinery*.[29] These are the most honorific awards given in the field of Computer Science for outstanding accomplishment. The winner presents a paper discussing the state of the discipline. I looked at efforts to define the type of knowledge in the field of Computer Science, to provide foundational statements for the discipline, to determine the ability of Computer Science to generate certain knowledge. While most of the papers did not go far in addressing these questions, they do express a general foundational theme: the field of Computer Science is characterized, no doubt uniquely, by a machine, the computer. Jack Carlson, in a letter to the journal in 1966, reveals his embarrassment about this aspect of the field: "The creation of computer science departments is . . . analogous to creating new departments for the railroad, automobile, radio, airplane, or television technologies."[30] Computer science is no doubt the only case in which a scientific field was established that focuses on a machine, and which defines itself as being so focused. While other sciences study nature or human beings, the language game of Computer Science is legitimized by a machinic narrative object, the computer.

The computer stands as the referent object to the discourse of Computer Science. As such it is in the position of the imaginary, the mirror of this science's false recognition and is invested with great signifying power, inscribed with transcendent status. I mean by this that Computer Science is to some degree dependent on computers in the way a child is dependent on its mother. The computer scientist cannot escape the relation to the computer; his or her identity is bound up with the computer. As the field of Computer Science develops, constituting the computer scientist in ever new ways through disciplinary practices, the relation to the computer remains one of misrecognition. Since Computer Science found its first identity through its relation to the computer, that identity remains part of the disciplinary protocol of the field, even if the actual object, the computer, changes significantly, even unrecognizably, in the course of the years.

Since computers are useful objects to industry and government, computer "scientists" are especially sensitive to the question of the epistemological purity of their discipline. Louis Fein, writing to the *Communications of the Association for Computing Machinery*, insistently articulates his distress with the ambiguous status of his field: "like other sciences, our science should maintain its sole abstract purpose of advancing truth and knowledge. It is not clear to me that an organization can play simultaneously the role of a profession, of an industry, and of a science."[31] What Computer Science requires then is a stable identity and this, as Maurice Wilkes, one of the Turing Award recipients, contends, can only be sustained through the machine: "what keeps us together is not some abstraction . . . but the actual hardware that we work with every day."[32] Or again another award winner, R. W. Hamming, admits that "at the heart of computer science lies a technological device, the computing machine."[33]

If the essence of Computer Science is a machine, how is the boundary between the science and the scientist to be drawn and maintained? In another letter, Peter Denning expresses just such an anxiety about loss of boundary between the machine and the computer scientist: "Without knowledge of the abstractions of computer science we run the immense risk of being unable to recognize when we are becoming the subjects of the instruments we created to be our subjects."[34] Allen Newell and Herbert A. Simon, Turing Award winners in 1976, precisely attempt to define Computer Science as the unity of man and machine: "The machine – not just the hardware, but the programmed, living machine – is the organism we study."[35] For them, however, language is material in a literal sense: "intelligence resides in physical symbol systems." And the interpretation of "language" is algorithmic: the simple "carrying out" of processes designated by programs. Language, in other words, is formulaic, at its best closed and unambiguous.

Computer Science then is a discourse at the border of words and things, a dangerous discipline because it is founded on the confusion between the scientist and his or her object. The identity of the scientist and the computer are so close that a mirror effect may very easily come into play: the scientist projects intelligent subjectivity onto the computer and the computer then becomes the criterion by which to define intelligence, judge the scientist, outline the essence of humanity. And indeed one Turing Award winner suggests exactly this. In 1987 John E. Hopcroft writes:

> The potential of computer science, if fully explored and developed, will take us to a higher plane of knowledge about the world. Computer science will assist us in gaining a greater understanding of intellectual processes. It will enhance our knowledge of the learning process, the thinking process, and the reasoning process. Computer science will provide models and conceptual tools for the cognitive sciences. Just as the physical sciences have dominated man's intellectual endeavors during this century as researchers explored the nature of matter and the beginning of the universe, today we are beginning the exploration of the intellectual universe of ideas, knowledge structures, and language.[36]

The imaginary foundation of computer science is here firmly in place, essentialized as a closed discourse whose domain is spirit. "Artificial intelligence" and human intelligence are doppelgangers, each imitating the other so closely that one scarcely can distinguish them.

The field of Computer Science is commonly viewed as bifurcated between hardware and software, between those whose central reference is the machine and those whose focus is artificial intelligence, between the engineers and the mathematicians. But this opposition, while important at one level, disguises a certain consensus concerning the man/machine relation. The electrification of science in the form of the computer generates a discourse at the border of mind and matter and in so doing destabilizes the distinction between the two. A volatile discursive situation haunts the field of Computer Science so that, though some fall on the side of the machine and others on the side of "intelligence," both camps reduce one side to the other and neither can sustain the difference very well. The engineers close off the field around the sign of the machine; the mathematicians do the same but around the sign of the mind. Hopcroft, illustrating the latter choice in the above passage, equates the language game of artificial intelligence with human knowledge itself. As we develop computer languages we are, he contends, not simply inventing new discourses but objectifying the human mind. The discourse of computer science is decidedly not postmodern in Lyotard's sense but firmly logocentric.

On a more prosaic but no less important level, computers are now crucial to industry and to the military, as Lyotard indicates, but also to science itself. The work of Mandelbrot, for instance, is inconceivable without computers. Both the science that is tied to performativity and the postmodern science of "little narratives" and "paralogy" depend on the computer for their functioning. A full study is needed of this dependence, of the ways the computer configures their research, of its power effects as a disciplinary discourse/practice, of its legitimation effects as a language game; one needs to reconstruct the marginalizing effects of its centering and essentializing textuality.

The Differend and Community

In the end *The Postmodern Condition* rests upon an intuition, a "weak" assertion[37] which appears to bother Lyotard perhaps more than it should. For Lyotard identifies himself as a "philosopher" (p. xxv), aligning himself with the long tradition that stretches back to Plato and the preSocratics. This tradition does not easily accommodate intuitions, judgments obviously open to dispute, statements that exceed themselves, that are unable to support their claims by ratiocination. Lyotard often registers his discomfort with the discipline of philosophy, complaining for instance about the coercive nature of the Platonic dialectic.[38] Yet he does not hesitate to define himself within the discipline of philosophy.

In *The Differend* Lyotard is even more insistent to define his status as a philosopher. He withdraws from some of what might be seen as the excesses of the earlier work and supplies argumentation that resembles that of a strictly philosophical presentation. The "phrase", for example, becomes a logically irreducible basis for any discourse, one which flows out of it in a recognizably "philosophical" manner. But if contemporary discourse is conditioned by a crisis of metanarratives, must not the position of the philosopher also be put in question, as it has been by a long line of thinkers starting at least with Marx and Nietzsche? A troubling ambiguity subverts Lyotard's text: he seeks the security of the standpoint of the philosopher while undermining its basis; he wants recognition as a philosopher but his argument refuses the epistemological status normally accorded to the philosopher.

By the end of *The Differend* a certain uneasiness disturbs the reader. Lyotard has made claims for a multiplicity of language games, for the justice of the acceptance of this multiplicity, in opposition to all arguments (especially Habermas's) for consensus, for totalizing unifications which reduce possible positions of enunciation. The claim for this postmodern effusion of difference is itself not one of these games but one that stands above the rest, a metastatement that legitimizes the proliferation of discourse. Lyotard is aware of this dilemma and it destabilizes his discourse especially because he has adopted the philosopher's mantle. The dilemma concerns, I believe, that of the white male theorist who supports the eruption of heterogeneity – the validation of the other that is typical of feminists and subaltern discourse – but who has no firm standpoint from which to assert that support. With *The Differend* the tension in Lyotard becomes acute as his position of enunciation more and more resembles that of the philosopher while his argument insists more and more systematically on legitimizing the incompatibility of differends.[39] It is a tension that is simply not reducible; perhaps it is in Derridean terms an undecidable.

Lyotard is in fact aware of the relation of philosophy to patriarchy and to feminist theory. In *Rudiments païens* he devotes a chapter to the question of patriarchy, citing Hélène Cixous and Luce Irigaray to support his position. He charges philosophy with the responsibility for the masculine/feminine distinction and shows how the discourse of philosophy is inseparable from patriarchy. Philosophy for him is a discourse of metastatements, as distinct from ordinary speech, and metastatements presume the male position, the social ground of the free association of men as it existed for example in ancient Greece. In this context, women represent a position of difference, a difference which must be repressed by philosophy. And so, Lyotard writes, "women can only be part of modern society if their differences are neutralized."[40] Women are thus in the position of what Lyotard later defines as the Differend. Yet in his work of the 1980s the theme of feminist critique, apparently so appropriate to Lyotard's concerns, does not surface in his work.

The Differend calls for a return to philosophy: "The time has come to philosophize," Lyotard proclaims.[41] This return is taken against his earlier book, which, as we have seen, is an essay in the sociology of knowledge, and also against poststructuralism in general which treats the philosophical tradition as a problem, not as a resort. Lyotard defines the philospher somewhat unconventionally as one who does not "presuppose the rules of his [*sic*] own discourse" (p. xiv) and explicitly distinguishes the philosopher from the theorist who presumably does so presuppose. The chief theme of the book is to philosophize "the Differend." Lyotard gives a definition of the Differend as incompatible difference, as "a case of conflict . . . that cannot be resolved for lack of a rule of judgment applicable to both arguments" (p. xi). What appears in *The Postmodern Condition* as the language game Lyotard now more rigorously thematizes as the Differend.

One example of the Differend that runs through the book is the suffering of the Jews at Auschwitz. Lyotard's discussion of Auschwitz is easily misunderstood and is perhaps not a wisely chosen case. But Auschwitz is important for him in illustrating certain features of the Differend; "the reality of the wrong suffered at Auschwitz before the foundation of [the state of Israel] remained and remains to be established, and it cannot be established because it is in the nature of a wrong not to be established by consensus" (p. 56). The reality of the difference in the Differend is by its nature non-adjudicable, and nothing illustrates this more for Lyotard than Auschwitz; "with Auschwitz, something new has happened in history . . . which is that the facts, the testimonies which bore the traces of *here's* and *now's*, the documents which indicated the sense or senses of the facts, and the names, finally the possibility of various kinds of phrases whose conjunction makes reality, all this has been destroyed as much as possible" (p. 57). Auschwitz then is the name of a wrong that cannot be "proven": "the historian must break with the monopoly over history granted to the cognitive regimen of phrases, and he or she must venture forth by lending his or her ear to what is not presentable under the rules of knowledge" (p. 57).

The Jews are important for Lyotard then as the boundary case of the modern. They define the limit of the modern in political theory since their injustice cannot be contained within theory. This argument is extended in the more recent *Heidegger et "les juifs"*. Here Lyotard argues that modern politics is characterized by a "terrorist" discourse which continually denies its lack of ground by repressing everything that suggests the lack. Modernism wins its legitimacy by "exterminating" everything which relativizes it. And the Jews play a tragic role in this language game: "insofar as the 'spirit' of the West has concerned itself with establishing its foundation, 'the Jews' are that which resists this spirit . . . They are that which cannot be domesticated within the obsession to dominate . . ."[43] The Jews are that which threaten the West with its lack of foundation, a reminder of insufficiency that cannot be integrated or repressed. To subvert the modern, to transgress its terrible boundary, one must find a way to undo its repression, find a way to present what is within its discursive constraints unpresentable.[43]

Later in the same book Lyotard charges the philosopher with this same task: to present the unpresentable. "Our responsibility before thought consists . . . in detecting differends and in finding the (impossible) idiom for phrasing them. This is what a philosopher does. An intellectual is someone who helps forget differends" (p. 142). Indeed much of the intellectual and philosophical community in Paris in the 1980s was obsessed with presenting one unpresentable in particular: German fascism. Derrida in *De l'Esprit: Heidegger et la question* (1987), Philippe Lacoue-Labarthe in *La fiction du politique* (1987), Lyotard himself in *Heidegger et 'les Juifs'* (1988), Pierre Bourdieu in a reprint of *L'Ontologie politique de Martin Heidegger* (1988), and many others delved into the issue of fascism, the meaning of the Holocaust, the question of Heidegger's (and therefore philosophy's) implication in Nazism. The fact of such an extraordinary confluence of interests might itself serve as an example of the unpresentable, or perhaps only of a little mystery of Paris. The coincidental discovery of Paul De Man's early writings for collaborationist Belgian periodicals added to the drama of the intellectual situation.[44] In the end Lyotard set aside for a future dispute among the faculties of philosophy and history the territorial question of the field of the unpresentable.

Despite Lyotard's avoidance of the topic of postmodernism in *The Differend*, certain themes from the earlier work reappear. Cognitive knowledge, in *The Differend*, remains "totalitarian." In both books the positivist view of knowledge is a form of terrorism that regulates reality and reduces or eliminates forms of being in the name of truth. Whether in computerized databases available for state surveillance or as metanarratives of science, cognitive knowledge delimits being as it claims merely to know it. Hence Lyotard's definition of the political as the Differend, as that which resists incorporation within "knowledge" – "Politics . . . is the threat of the Differend" (p. 138) – and hence too the privileged position of Auschwitz as the wrong which cannot be "known." And if a continuity is found with regard to knowledge, so too persists the theme of freedom as the recognition of multiplicity, heterogeneity, difference. The new focus in *The Differend* is the issue of linkage between heterogeneous beings and phrases.

The question of linkage poses the final issue of this study: the question of community in the mode of information. The traditions of critical social theory have advocated the elimination of domination from the social field with the aim of fostering a transparent community, a field in which human beings regulate their relations with as little interference as possible by socially created hierarchies or asymmetries. Domination institutes blocks and barriers between individuals and groups; it divides society into classes producing conflict and antagonism. In a recent discussion of the theme of community among critical social theorists, a strong sense emerged that the Marxist dream of community as a self-regulating association of producers, or more broadly, any image of utopia as individual realization through tightknit, face-to-face community must be abandoned because it is an obsolete piece of nostalgia.[45]

Lyotard criticizes the Marxist notion of community on the ground that community is, in Kantian terms, an idea not a concept. Marx mistakenly thinks he can erect a model of community in theory which can be realized through social action. However "community" is not cognitive but ethico-political. It requires normative statements, not descriptive ones. "Revolutionary politics," Lyotard charges, "rests upon a transcendental illusion in the political realm: it confuses what is presentable as an object for a speculative and/or ethical phrase; that is, it confuses schemata or exempla with *analoga* . . ."[46] Community remains, for the postmodern critic, a nonpresentable norm which cannot be rationally legitimized, only asserted by political means within discourse. But this critique of community depends upon a questionable Kantian distinction between cognitive and ethical statements, one that is not satisfactorily resolved by Lyotard.

Lyotard also departs from the communitarian tradition by contending that the effort of harmony and consensus is a form of domination, while division and antagonism allows the free development of opposing discursive groups. In the context of the politics of the 1970s and 1980s, with the emergence of diverse centers of protest, Lyotard's position in favor of multiplicity deserves attention. In addition the mode of information, with its discursive constitution of multiple, decentered and dispersed subjects, supports the anti-totalizing aspect of the Differend. Yet the political question of conflict between quasi-autonomous discursive positions or differends remains unresolved. Lyotard takes one important step in the direction of postmodern politics, one that refuses the unifying tendency of Jacobin and Bolshevik modernity. The next step remains unclear. Surely Lyotard's recommendaiton at the end of *The Postmodern Condition* to "give the public free access to the memory and data banks" (p. 67), while salutary in itself, does not advance very far in the direction of postmodern justice.

A more comprehensive treatment of the issue of postmodern politics will have to face the question of the disintegrating impulses of the mode of information. It is one thing to argue for a community of multiplicity; it is another to face the impossibility of community altogether. Critical social theory assumed a community base of face-to-face interactions, assumed a minimal network of spoken communications. The community was a palpable (male?) social force in the Jacobin clubs of 1789, and before that in "Literary circles and societies, masonic lodges, academies, and patriotic and cultural clubs . . .",[47] in the workers councils of 1917, the coffee houses and taverns of bourgeois and working-class culture of the past two centuries. Electronically mediated communication to some degree supplements existing forms of sociability but to another extent substitutes for them. New and unrecognizable modes of community are in the process of formation and it is difficult to discern exactly how these will contribute to or detract from postmodern politics. The image of the people in the streets, from the Bastille in 1789, to the Sorbonne in 1968 and Tiananmen Square, Beijing in 1989 may be the images that will not be repeated in the forms of upheaval of the twenty-first century and beyond.

Notes

Introduction

1 See *Los Angeles Times* articles on November 9, 23 and 25.
2 John Markoff, "Computer Viruses Thwart the Experts," *International Herald Tribune*, June 9, 1989, p. 12.
3 Paul Brodeur, "Annals of Radiation: The Hazards of Electromagnetic Fields, III – Video Display Terminals," *New Yorker*, June 26, 1989, pp. 39ff.
4 *New York Times*, October 18, 1987. See also reports in the *Times* on the earlier and smaller collapse on September 12, 1986 where it was noted that "wide use of computers contributed to the slide."
5 Marvin, Carolyn, *When Old Technologies Were New: Thinking About Electric Communication in the Late Nineteenth Century* (New York: Oxford University Press, 1988), p. 4.
6 Ibid., pp. 107, 162.
7 Ibid., p. 190.
8 Luigi Albertini, *The Origins of the War of 1914*, trans. and ed. Isabella Massey (New York: Oxford, 1952–7), vol. 2, ch. 4, pp. 120–79, for the details of these events.
9 For a strong argument to this effect see Elizabeth Eisenstein, *The Printing Press as an Agent of Change: Communications and Cultural Transformations in Early-Modern Europe* (New York: Cambridge University Press, 1979).
10 This term has been fruitfully developed by Anthony Giddens in his recent books. See for example *The Nation State and Violence* (Cambridge: Polity, 1986).

11 The leading purveyor of this point of view is *The Absolute Sound* with its intrepid editor, Harry Pearson. This "underground" audiophile journal has, since the late 1970s, pursued the quest for the perfect representation of music in the home. In an evaluation of an amplifier (which, by the way, costs $5,000), the reviewer praised the component as "mightily akin to the real thing. ... You will find yourself playing and replaying familiar recordings [on the amplifier,] ... basking in the true representation ... One can [when using this amplifier] easily pinpoint the location of each musical source ... on both the lateral and depth planes. In addition, the image size is correctly maintained, as are the separating spaces between the instruments. Remarkably, not only are there detectable spaces between the musical sources, but the size of these separating spaces ... is also captured by this amplifier." John Nork, "A Tale of Three Amplifiers," *The Absolute Sound*, 13:55, September/October 1988, p. 56. For another sample of this point of view see William Semple, "The Absolute Sound Itself," *The Absolute Sound*, 8:30, June 1983, pp. 26–32, in which the tonal qualities of concert halls are examined.

12 His actual words are "man would be erased, like a face drawn in sand at the edge of the sea." Michel Foucault, *The Order of Things: An Archaeology of the Human Sciences* (New York: Pantheon, 1970), p. 387.

13 For an excellent analysis of Cartesian culture as masculine see Susan Bordo, *The Flight into Objectivity: Essays on Cartesianism and Culture* (Albany: State University of New York Press, 1987).

14 See the fascinating discussion of money and writing in Gayatri Spivak, "Speculations on Reading Marx: After Reading Derrida," in Derek Attridge et al., eds, *Poststructuralism and the Question of History* (New York: Cambridge University Press, 1987), pp. 30–62.

15 Fredric Jameson, *The Political Unconscious* (Ithaca: Cornell University Press, 1981), pp. 60–1.

16 Richard Terdiman, *Discourse/Counter-Discourse: The Theory and Practice of Symbolic Resistance in Nineteenth-Century France* (Ithaca: Cornell University Press, 1985), p. 43.

17 Gilles Deleuze and Félix Guattari, *Anti-Oedipus: Capitalism and Schizophrenia*, trans. Robert Hurley, Mark Seem and Helen Lane (Minneapolis: University of Minnesota Press, 1983), and *A Thousand Plateaus: Capitalism and Schizophrenia*, trans.

Brian Massumi (Minneapolis: University of Minnesota Press, 1987).

18 Teilhard de Chardin, *The Phenomenon of Man*, trans. Bernard Wall (New York: Harper and Row, 1961).

19 For an illuminating discussion of these issues see Dana Polan, "Brief Encounters: Mass Culture and the Evacuation of Sense," in Tania Modleski, ed., *Studies in Entertainment: Critical Approaches to Mass Culture* (Bloomington: University of Indiana Press, 1986), pp. 167–87.

20 See the excellent discussion of this theme in Andreas Huyssen, "Mass Culture as Woman: Modernism's Other," in Modleski, ed., *Studies in Entertainment*, pp. 188–207.

21 Feminist theorists have also moved in this direction. See for example Julia Kristeva, *Revolution in Poetic Language*, trans. Margaret Waller (New York: Columbia University Press, 1984), and *Desire in Language: A Semiotic Approach to Literature and Art*, trans. Thomas Gora et al. (New York: Columbia University Press, 1980); Hélène Cixous and Catherine Clement, *The Newly Born Woman*, trans. Betsy Wing (Minneapolis: University of Minnesota Press, 1986); Luce Irigaray, *This Sex Which Is Not One*, trans. Catherine Porter (Ithaca: Cornell University Press, 1985). For an interesting argument on this score see Leslie Rabine, "A Feminist Politics of Non-Identity," *Feminist Studies*, 14:1, Spring 1988, pp. 11–31.

22 This strategy develops further the models of David Carroll and Suzanne Gearhart who combine theoretic and empirical material playing each off against the other.

Chapter 1   The Concept of Postindustrial Society

1 The first use of the term postindustrial society, to my knowledge, is found in Alain Touraine, *La Société post-industrielle: Naissance d'une société* (Paris: Denoël, 1969). Touraine uses the term to define new radical forces rather than to analyze the social structure *per se*. Thus it is Daniel Bell who first used the term in the way that defines the debate. See his "Notes on the Post Industrial Society," *Public Interest*, 6 and 7, Winter and Spring 1967, pp. 24–35 and 102–18. For an interesting overview of theories of postindustrial or information society see David Lyon, *The Information Society: Issues and Illusions* (Cambridge: Polity, 1988) and Boris Frankel, *The Post-Industrial Utopians* (Madison: University of Wisconsin Press, 1987).

2   Daniel Bell, "The Social Framework of the Information Society" in Tom Forester, ed., *The Microelectronics Revolution* (Oxford: Blackwell, 1980), p. 521. Also by Forester is *High-Tech Society: The Story of the Information Technology Revolution* (Boston: MIT Press, 1987). For an effort to measure increases in "knowledge" see Fritz Machlup, *The Production and Distribution of Knowledge in the United States* (Princeton: Princeton University Press, 1962).

3   For a critique of Bell's position on the economy, along with a gloomy assessment of the prospects of an information society, see Jonathan Gershunny, *After Industrial Society?: The Emerging Self-service Economy* (New York: Macmillan, 1978), and with I. D. Miles, *The New Service Economy: The Transformation of Employment in Industrial Societies* (London: Pinter, 1983).

4   Daniel Bell, "Social Framework," p. 501. See also Bell, *The Coming of Postindustrial Society* (New York: Basic Books, 1973), p. 343.

5   Bell, *Coming of Postindustrial Society*, p. 487.

6   In the sequel to *The Coming of Postindustrial Society, The Cultural Contradictions of Capitalism* (New York: Harper and Row, 1976), Bell specifies the dynamic conflict of contemporary society as a rift between axial principles (cultural hedonism vs. democratic politics and postindustrial social structure). The position is in sharp contrast with the reductive rhetoric of the earlier work where the social structure (postindustrial society) absorbed the other axial principles.

7   Bell, "Social Framework," p. 532.

8   Ibid., p. 507.

9   Ibid., p. 506.

10 The term "performative" is taken from J. L. Austin, *How to Do Things With Words* (Cambridge, Mass.: Harvard University Press, 1962). Performatives may be defined as acts in the guise of words. In Austin's book they are words whose effects do not conform to the conventional definition of meaning as the correspondence of word and thing.

11 See Cornélius Castoriadis, *L'institution imaginaire de la société* (Paris: Editions du Seuil, 1975), for an important elaboration of the role of figurative imagination in social theory. The problem in Bell's discourse is not that he uses figures, but that he presents them as rational, scientific determinations, thereby confounding the register of his discourse and introducing performatives.

12 This of course is not true of all social scientists. Throughout this study I indicate my debt to many who have initiated this problematic before me. In political science, Michael J. Shapiro, to mention one name, has worked in this direction as for example in *The Politics of Representation: Writing Practices in Biography, Photography and Policy Analysis* (Madison: University of Wisconsin Press, 1988.) In organization theory, see Robert Cooper and Gibson Burrell, "Modernism, Postmodernism and Organizational Analysis: An Introduction," *Organization Studies*, 9:1, 1988, pp. 91–112. In sociology see Norman Denzin, "Postmodern Social Theory," *Sociological Theory*, 4, fall 1986, pp. 194–204. In geography see E. W. Soja, *Postmodern Geographies: The Reassertion of Space in Critical Social Theory* (London: Verso, 1989). I am grateful to Pauline Vaillancourt-Rosenau for informing me about some of these titles.

13 See for example Dallas W. Smythe, "Communications: Blindspot of Western Marxism," *Canadian Journal of Political and Social Theory*, 1 (3), Fall 1977, pp. 1–27, who calls for Marxists to pay attention to communications but suggests an economic reductionist method for doing so. Along the same lines see Phil Blackburn, Ken Green and Sonia Liff, "Science and Technology in Restructuring," *Capital and Class*, 18, Winter 1982, pp. 15–37.

14 The prime axiom of Marxist economic theory, the labor theory of value, equally does not apply in the age of information. As Marx himself noted in the *Grundrisse*, once science enters the production process the law of value is undone. It becomes impossible to determine the exact proportion that each worker contributes to the production of wealth.

15 There are many studies and discussions of the new laws required to incorporate information within the market system and to protect the civil rights of individuals. See for example Gary Marx, "The New Surveillance," *Technology Review*, May–June, 1985, pp. 43–8; David Burnham, *The Rise of the Computer State* (New York: Random House, 1983); James B. Rule, *Private Lives and Public Surveillance: Social Control in the Computer Age* (New York: Schocken, 1974).

16 I do not of course mean to exclude completely the economic dimension of the analysis of information.

17 Bell, *Coming of Postindustrial Society*, p. 172. See also "Social Framework," p. 509. Brian Winston, *Misunderstanding Media*

(New York: Routledge and Kegan Paul, 1986) is critical of what he sees as Bell's rosy view of the impact of the media.

18   Bell, "Social Framework," p. 509.

19   Norbert Wiener, *The Human Use of Human Beings: Cybernetics and Society* (New York: Anchor, 1954), p. 15. The problem of centralized control afforded by cybernetic technology is criticized by Abbe Mowshowitz, *The Conquest of Will: Information Processing in Human Affairs* (Menlo Park: Addison Wesley, 1976). See also Harlan Cleveland, "The Twilight of Hierarchy: Speculations on the Global Information Society," in Bruce Guile, ed., *Information Technologies and Social Transformation* (Washington, D.C.: National Academy Press, 1985), pp. 55–79.

20   Wiener, *Human Use*, p. 17.

21   Ibid.

22   See Bell, *Cultural Contradictions*, and Larry Hirschhorn, *Beyond Mechanization: Work and Technology in a Postindustrial Age* (Cambridge, Mass.: MIT, 1984).

23   See the review of *Beyond Mechanization* by Rob Kling in *Science*, 230 (4729), November 29, 1985, pp. 1031–2.

24   This is an important phenomenon that has not been investigated enough. See Langdon Winner, *Autonomous Technology: Technics-out-of-Control as a Theme in Political Thought* (Cambridge, Mass.: MIT, 1977), for a discussion of the theme of fragility in advanced technological societies. In *The Whale and the Reactor: A Search for Limits in an Age of High Technology* (Chicago: University of Chicago Press, 1986) Winner expands this analysis to focus on the way knowledge has become political in the mode of information.

25   Richard Terdiman, *Discourse/Counter-Discourse: The Theory and Practice of Symbolic Resistance in Nineteenth-Century France* (Ithaca: Cornell University Press, 1985), makes this argument in a fascinating analysis of French newspapers in the nineteenth century.

26   Karl Marx, *Grundrisse: Introduction to the Critique of Political Economy*, trans. Martin Nicolaus (New York: Random House, 1973), p. 704.

27   Ibid., p. 705.

28   Ibid.

29   Ibid.

30   Ibid., p. 706.

31   Ibid.

32   Max Horkheimer and Theodor Adorno, *Dialectic of Enlighten-*

ment, trans. John Cumming (New York: Seabury, 1972), especially "Excursus I: Odysseus or Myth and Enlightenment."

33 See Herbert Marcuse, *Reason and Revolution: Hegel and the Rise of Social Theory* (Boston: Beacon, 1960). Originally published in 1941.

34 *Telos*, 19, Spring 1974, pp. 13–90.

35 Reprinted in Andrew Arato and Eike Gebhardt, eds, *The Essential Frankfurt School Reader* (New York: Urizen, 1978), pp. 270–99.

36 "How to Look at Television," *Quarterly of Film, Radio and Television*, 8, 1954, pp. 213–55. Reprinted as "Television and the Patterns of Mass Culture," in Bernard Rosenberg and David White, eds, *Mass Culture* (Glencoe: Free Press, 1957), pp. 474–87.

37 For Adorno's critique of positivism, see Theodor Adorno et al., *The Positivist Dispute in German Sociology*, trans. Glyn Adey and David Frisby (New York: Harper and Row, 1976). Originally published in 1969.

38 See Michel Foucault, *Power/Knowledge: Selected Interviews and Other Writings, 1972–1977*, trans. and ed. Colin Gordon (New York: Pantheon, 1980), for the best statements of his position.

39 The essay was dedicated to Herbert Marcuse and later translated in Jürgen Habermas, *Toward a Rational Society*, trans. Jeremy Shapiro (Boston: Beacon, 1970; also Cambridge: Polity).

40 Ibid., p. 90.

41 Max Weber, *Economy and Society: An Outline of Interpretive Sociology*, ed. Guenther Roth and Claus Wittich (Berkeley: University of California Press, 1978), vol. 1, p. 4.

42 Such as the personal bondage of feudal societies in which domination was legitimated by means of traditional action. As long as action was based on the authority of the past, reason was preempted since there could be no question of the individual's capacity to choose. Individuals had the capacity to judge if an action conformed to pre-existing types of action and was thereby legitimate; but they were presumed not have the capacity to judge if an action was in their own best interests, or at least this basis for action was not considered legitimate. Weber's point is that feudal bondage could not operate if instrumental reason was a legitimate basis for action. Thus a social system that legitimates the personal domination of one individual over another is incompatible with rational action.

And therefore the great hope of modern society is that it abolishes personal domination since it institutes instrumental action.

43 This dilemma is explicitly recognized by Weber in his discussions of the social revolution in Russia. See *Economy and Society*, vol. 1, p. 225 and *passim*.

44 "'Objectivity' in Social Science and Social Policy," in Max Weber, *The Methodology of the Social Sciences*, trans. and ed. Edward Shils and Henry Finch (New York: Free Press, 1949). In Weber's words, "An 'ideal type' in our sense ... has no connection at all with *value-judgments* ..." (p. 98).

45 "Science as a Vocation," in *From Max Weber: Essays in Sociology*, trans. and ed. H. Gerth and C. Wright Mills (New York: Oxford, 1958), p. 144 *passim*.

46 Max Weber, *Economy and Society*, vol. 1, p. 225.

47 A parallel critique of Weber may be found in Jürgen Habermas, *The Theory of Communicative Action*, vol. 1: *Reason and the Rationalization of Society*, trans. Thomas McCarthy (Boston: Beacon, 1984; also Cambridge: Polity), pp. 143–271.

48 Ibid.

49 *Toward a Rational Society*, p. 96.

50 Ibid., p. 98.

51 For a full discussion of this issue see Jürgen Habermas, *Legitimation Crisis*, trans. Thomas McCarthy (Boston: Beacon, 1975; also Cambridge: Polity).

52 *Toward a Rational Society*, p. 115.

53 This concept is elaborated in Jürgen Habermas, *Communication and the Evolution of Society*, trans. Thomas McCarthy (Boston: Beacon, 1979; also Cambridge; Polity).

54 Ibid., p. 97

55 Ibid., pp. 154–8.

56 *Reason and the Rationalization of Society*, p. 179.

Chapter 2   Baudrillard and TV Ads

1 Niklas Luhmann, "Generalized Media and the Problem of Contingency," in Jan Loubser et al., eds, *Explorations in General Theory in Social Science* (New York: Free Press, 1976), vol. 2, p. 512. In the same collection, see also Rainer C. Baum, "Communication and Media," in *Explorations*, vol. 2, pp. 533–56. For an evaluation and critique of sociological views on the media see Tod Gitlin, "Media Sociology: The Dominant

Paradigm," *Theory and Society*, 6, 1978, pp. 205ff. For an argument that new tools are needed to "read" television see John Fiske and John Hartley, *Reading Television* (London: Methuen, 1978).

2   See Erving Goffman, *The Presentation of Self in Everyday Life* (New York: Doubleday, 1959) and *Interaction Ritual: Essays on Face-to-Face Behavior* (New York: Anchor, 1967).

3   Joshua Meyrowitz, *No Sense of Place: The Impact of Electronic Media on Social Behavior* (New York: Oxford, 1985), p. 6.

4   Ibid., p. 314.

5   Ibid., p. 70.

6   For a fine analysis of the way newscasts constitute their audience/subjects see Margaret Morse, "The Television News Personality and Credibility," in Tania Modleski, ed., *Studies in Entertainment: Critical Approaches to Mass Culture* (Bloomington: University of Indiana Press, 1986), pp. 55–79.

7   In a study of white, affluent families in Orange County, California in 1986, I found that respondents lied in the questionnaire most often about time spent watching TV. Among all the topics in a lengthy questionnaire, some of which concerned intimate issues, respondents had most difficulty admitting that they watched TV as often as they did.

8   Roland Marchand, *Advertising and the American Dream: Making Way for Modernity, 1920–1940* (Berkeley: University of California Press, 1985) is a very fine example of this type of analysis. The book provides numerous insights into the changing definition of the modern, as does his unpublished essay, "Contested Terrain: *Where* Do Consumers and Advertisers Meet?"

9   Christopher Lasch exemplifies the moral outrage of critics of TV ads in *Haven in a Heartless World: The Family Besieged* (New York: Basic, 1977), p. 19 *passim*.

10   Marchand, *Advertising*, p. 11.

11   Vance Packard, *The Hidden Persuaders* (New York: D. McKay, 1964).

12   For an excellent analysis of the psychological effect of TV, posited as the opposite of the centered subject, see Beverle Houston, "Viewing Television: The Metapsychology of Endless Consumption," *Quarterly Review of Film Studies*, Summer 1984, pp. 183–95. I am indebted to David James for telling me about this essay.

13   T. J. Jackson Lears and Richard Wightman Fox, eds, *The*

Culture of Consumption: Critical Essays in American History, 1880–1980 (New York: Pantheon, 1983), p. xii.

14 T. J. Jackson Lears, "From Salvation to Self-Realization: Advertising and the Therapeutic Roots of Consumer Culture, 1880-1930," in *Culture of Consumption*, p. 21.

15 Ibid., p. 22.

16 Ibid., p. 16.

17 The exception is the promising work of Nick Browne, particularly in "The Political Economy of the Television (Super) Text," *Quarterly Review of Film Studies*, Summer 1984, pp. 174–82.

18 Another line of leftist criticism points to the resistance of audiences to the advertising message. See Kathy Peiss, *Cheap Amusements: Working Women and Leisure in Turn-of-the-Century New York* (Philadelphia: Temple University Press, 1986); Susan Porter Benson, *Counter Cultures: Saleswomen, Managers and Customers in American Department Stores, 1890–1940* (Urbana: University of Illinois Press, 1986); Roy Rosenzweig, *Eight Hours for What We Will: Workers and Leisure in an Industrial City, 1870–1920* (New York: Cambridge University Press, 1983); Francis Couvares, *The Remaking of Pittsburgh: Class and Culture in an Industrializing City, 1877–1919* (Albany: SUNY Press, 1984); and Janice Radway, *Reading the Romance: Women, Patriarchy and Popular Literature* (Chapel Hill: University of North Carolina Press, 1984). While these works document a certain resilience of working-class culture to the incursions of capitalist lures, too great a stress on this evidence leads to the danger of romanticizing a world that has no doubt sadly succumbed to the desocialization of the mode of information.

19 Louis Althusser, "Ideology and Ideological State Apparatuses (Notes Toward an Investigation)," in *Lenin and Philosophy and Other Essays*, trans. Ben Brewster (London: New Left Books, 1971), p. 136n.

20 Ibid., p. 153.

21 Ibid., p. 155.

22 Ibid., p. 160.

23 For further development of this line of critique see Teresa de Lauretis, *Technologies of Gender: Essays on Theory, Film, and Fiction* (Bloomington: Indiana University Press, 1987).

24 Althusser, "Ideology," p. 160.

25 Ibid., p. 172.

26 Ibid., p. 130.

27 For a selection of Baudrillard's writings in English see Mark Poster, ed., *Jean Baudrillard: Selected Writings*, trans. Jacques Mourrain (Cambridge: Polity; Stanford: Stanford University Press, 1988), and for a review of Baudrillard's thought see Douglas Kellner, *Jean Baudrillard: From Marxism to Postmodernism and Beyond* (Cambridge: Polity; Stanford: Stanford University Press, 1989).

28 Ferdinand de Saussure, *Course in General Linguistics*, ed. Charles Belly and Albert Sechehaye, trans. Wade Baskin (New York: Philosophical Library, 1959).

29 Raymond Williams is unusual among Marxists in attempting to account for the impact of linguistic structures on their own terms. See *Television: Technology and Cultural Form* (London: Fontana, 1974) and as editor, *Contact: Human Communication and its History* (London: Thames and Hudson, 1981).

30 Roland Barthes, *The Fashion System*, trans. Matthew Ward and Richard Howard (New York: Hill and Wang, 1983), p. 288. Originally published in 1967.

31 Ibid., p. 234.

32 Rosalind H. Williams, *Dream Worlds: Mass Consumption in Late Nineteenth-Century France* (Berkeley: University of California Press, 1982) for a detailed history of this process. Also of interest is Michael Miller, *The Bon Marché: Bourgeois Culture and the Department Store, 1869–1920* (Princeton: Princeton University Press, 1981).

33 Roland Barthes, *Mythologies*, sel. and trans. Annette Lavers (New York: Hill and Wang, 1972), first edition 1957.

34 Barthes, *Fashion System*, p. 286.

35 Ibid., p. 286.

36 Jean Baudrillard, *The Mirror of Production*, trans. Mark Poster (New York: Telos, 1975), pp. 120ff.

37 In English see, for example, Henri Lefebvre, *Everyday Life in the Modern World*, trans. Sacha Rabinovitch (New York: Harper and Row, 1971), pp. 110ff.

38 Richard Terdiman, *Discourse/Counter-Discourse: The Theory and Practice of Symbolic Resistance in Nineteenth-Century France* (Ithaca: Cornell University Press, 1985).

39 The argument here is different from that of Marshall McLuhan, for example in *Understanding Media: The Extensions of Man* (New York: McGraw-Hill, 1964) where emphasis is given not to language but to the sensorium, to perceptual processes.

40 Jean Baudrillard, *Simulations*, trans. Paul Foss et al. (New York: Semiotext(e), 1983), p. 2.
41 Ibid., pp. 147–8. Emphasis in original.
42 Gerry Gill, "Post-Structuralism as Ideology," *Arena*, 69, 1984, p. 70.
43 Ibid., p. 73.
44 Ibid., p. 75.
45 Ibid., p. 90.
46 Ibid., p. 93.
47 Ibid., p. 94.
48 This becomes a prominent theme in his writing from the late 1970s on. See for example Jean Baudrillard, *Les Stratégies fatales* (Paris: Bernard Grasset, 1983) and "The Masses: The Implosion of the Social in the Media," trans. Marie Maclean, *New Literary History*, 16 (3), Spring 1985, pp. 577–89.
49 Jean Baudrillard, "The Implosion of Meaning in the Media and the Implosion of the Social in the Masses," in Kathleen Woodward, ed., *The Mythos of Information: Technology and Postindustrial Culture* (Madison: Coda, 1980), p. 145.

Chapter 3 Foucault and Databases

1 Jack Goody, *The Domestication of the Savage Mind* (New York: Cambridge, 1977), p. 79.
2 David Godfrey and Douglas Parkhill, *Gutenberg Two* (1979) (Toronto: Porcépic, 1980), p. 1.
3 David Burnham, *The Rise of the Computer State* (New York: Random House, 1983), p. 42.
4 James B. Rule, *Private Lives and Public Surveillance: Social Control in the Computer Age* (New York: Schocken, 1974), p. 273.
5 See the notice of this new technology in *US News and World Report*, May 20, 1985, p. 16.
6 Another example of modern control capability is reported by Gary Marx: "The National Security Agency can simultaneously monitor 54,000 telephone transmissions to and from the United States." See "The New Surveillance," *Technology Review*, May/June 1985, p. 45, and also "I'll Be Watching You", *Dissent*, Winter 1985, pp. 26–34.
7 Michael A. Arbib, *Computers and the Cybernetic Society*, 2nd edn (New York: Academic, 1984), pp. 168–72.

8   Although before the industrial revolution most products were produced for use rather than for the market.

9   The same scenario is being reproduced with digital audio cassette recorders, "DAT"s. Available in Japan and Western Europe since 1986, the music industry in the United States thus far has prevented their importation. DATs enable the consumer to make exact copies of digitally encoded compact discs. Record manufacturers fear loss of sales and have lobbied effectively to deny consumers access to the new technology.

10 For an extensive account of these services and their implications for democratic society see Kevin G. Wilson, *Technologies of Control: The New Interactive Media for the Home* (Madison: University of Wisconsin Press, 1988).

11 Ibid., p. 35.

12 See *Domestication*, p. 68ff.

13 Harold A. Innis, *Empire and Communications*, ed. Mary Q. Innis (Toronto: University of Toronto Press, 1972), p. 7. Original version 1950.

14 Among McLuhan's works see *Understanding Media: The Extensions of Man* (New York: McGraw-Hill, 1964).

15 Anthony Giddens, *Social Theory and Modern Sociology* (Cambridge: Polity; Stanford: Stanford University Press, 1987), p. 100.

16 Ibid.

17 For examples of this position see Edgar Morin, Claude Lefort and Jean-Marc Courdray [aka Cornélius Castoriadis], *Mai 1968: la Brèche, premières réflexions sur les événements* (Paris: Fayard, 1968).

18 Ithiel de Sola Pool, *Technologies of Freedom* (Cambridge, Mass.: Harvard University Press, 1983), p. 251.

19 Yoneji Masuda, *The Information Society as Post-Industrial Society* (Washington, DC: World Future Society, 1981), p. 25. See also Hans Magnus Enzensberger, *The Consciousness Industry: On Literature, Politics and the Media* (New York: Seabury, 1974).

20 See Charles H. Cooley, *Social Organization; A Study of the Larger Mind* (New York: Scribner's, 1909), p. 23.

21 Goody, *Domestication*, pp. 68–70.

22 For more examples see *Newsweek*, March 17, 1986, p. 71.

23 Michel Foucault, "Two Lectures," trans. Colin Gordon et al., in Colin Gordon, ed., *Power/Knowledge: Selected Interviews*

and Other Writings, 1972–1977 (New York: Pantheon, 1980), p. 93.

24 Max Weber, *The Methodology of the Social Sciences*, trans. and ed. E. Shils and H. Finch (New York: Free Press, 1949), p. 59. See also "Science as a Vocation," to be found in *From Max Weber: Essays in Sociology*, trans. and ed. H. Gerth and C. W. Mills (New York: Oxford, 1958), pp. 129–56.

25 Michel Foucault, *Discipline and Punish*, trans. Alan Sheridan (New York: Pantheon, 1977), p. 24.

26 Ibid., p. 217.

27 For a history of this process see Rosalind H. Williams, *Dream Worlds: Mass Consumption in Late Nineteenth-Century France* (Berkeley: University of California Press, 1982).

28 See the fascinating discussion of controversies over the authenticity of various printed editions of the Bible in Jane O. Newman, "The Word Made Print: Luther's 1522 *New Testament* in an Age of Mechanical Reproduction," *Representations*, 11, Summer 1985, pp. 95–133.

29 I am indebted to Leslie Rabine for pointing out this aspect of the change in technologies of book production.

30 Foucault, *Discipline and Punish*, pp. 220–1.

31 Ibid., p. 220.

32 Jean-François Lyotard, *The Postmodern Condition: A Report on Knowledge*, trans. Geoff Bennington and Brian Massumi (Minneapolis: University of Minnesota Press, 1984), p. 67.

Chapter 4 Derrida and Electronic Writing

1 Gregory Ulmer, *Applied Grammatology: Post(e)-Pedagogy from Jacques Derrida to Joseph Beuys* (Baltimore: Johns Hopkins University Press, 1985), p. 303.

2 Ibid., p. 36.

3 Jacques Derrida, *Of Grammatology*, trans. Gayatri Spivak (Baltimore: Johns Hopkins University Press, 1974), pp. 86–7.

4 Jacques Derrida, *Positions*, trans. Alan Bass (Chicago: University of Chicago Press, 1981), p. 13.

5 Jacques Derrida, "Philosophie des états généraux," *Etats généraux de philosophie* (Paris: Flammarion, 1979), pp. 32, 38, 39, 40, 41. In addition Derrida briefly responded approvingly to Régis Debray's talk. See pp. 169–70.

6 Ibid., p. 41.

7 Conference on Annotation, UC Irvine, April 10, 1988.

8   Dominick LaCapra, "Of Lumpers and Readers," *Intellectual History Newsletter* 10 1988, p. 5. For an excellent discussion of the relation of text to context see Gregory Jay, "Values and Deconstructions: Derrida, Saussure, Marx," *Cultural Critique*, 8, Winter 1987–8, pp. 153–96.

9   Jacques Derrida, *Margins of Philosophy*, trans. Alan Bass (Chicago: University of Chicago Press, 1982), p. 318.

10 Derrida's position, as commentators have noted, is unusually difficult to summarize. It even calls into question, by its continual shifting of terms, the practice of paraphrase. An important debate among intellectual historians on this issue may be seen in Dominick LaCapra, "Rethinking Intellectual History and Reading Texts," in Dominick LaCapra and Steven Kaplan, eds, *Modern European Intellectual History: Reappraisals and New Perspectives* (Ithaca: Cornell University Press, 1982), pp. 47–85, and the response by Martin Jay in "Two Cheers for Paraphrase: The Confessions of a Synoptic Intellectual Historian," *Stanford Literary Review*, Spring 1986, pp. 46–61. Despite the dangers inherent in summarizing deconstruction, some efforts have succeeded. One such example is Christopher Norris, *Derrida* (Cambridge: Harvard University Press, 1987).

11 Some of these terms are hymen, pharmakon, fold, supplement, dissemination.

12 For Derrida's text see especially "Géopsychanalyse 'and the rest of the world,'" in *Psyché: Inventions de l'autre* (Paris: Galilée, 1987). See also Michael Ryan, *Marxism and Deconstruction: A Critical Articulation* (Baltimore: Johns Hopkins University Press, 1982). Fredric Jameson acknowledges the usefulness of deconstruction without giving up on Marxism in *The Political Unconscious: Narrative as a Social Symbolic Act* (Ithaca: Cornell University Press, 1981). Also suggestive on this account is Roberto Unger, *Social Theory, its Situation and its Task* (New York: Cambridge University Press, 1987), and *Politics: A Work of Constructive Social Theory* (New York: Cambridge University Press, 1987). Although Unger uses none of the terms of poststructuralism, he calls for a radicalization of destabilizing institutional routines and habits that bears great resemblance to the work of deconstructionists on texts.

13 Friedrich Nietzsche, *Thus Spake Zarathustra*, trans. Thomas Common (New York: Random House, n.d.), p. 11.

14 Jacques Derrida, *Writing and Difference*, trans. Alan Bass (Chicago: University of Chicago Press, 1978), p. 293.

15 *Of Grammatology*, p. 5.

16 Ibid., p. 4.

17 Jacques Derrida, *Dissemination*, trans. Barbara Johnson (Chicago: University of Chicago Press, 1981), p. 33.

18 Derrida returns to the theme of monsters, this time "theoretical" monsters in "Some Statements and Truisms About Neologisms, Newisms, Post-isms, Parasitisms, and Other Small Seismisms," in David Carroll, ed., *The States of Theory* (New York: Columbia University Press, 1989). Here Derrida shifts the designation "monster" to include totalizing positions. These are "normal monstrosities," as distinguished from "monstrous monstrosities," like deconstruction, "which never present themselves *as such*" and which are always "unrecognized and misunderstood." Derrida now drops the reference to the situation or new age as a monster but repeats this characterization of his own position. The characterization is paradoxical, to say the least, since at the same time as he refers to his position as a "monster" he asserts that "monsters" never present themselves *as such*. His presentation has normalized the monster and thus not represented it.

19 See Leslie Rabine, "A Feminist Politics of Non-Identity," *Feminist Studies*, 14 (1), Spring 1988, pp. 11–31, and Alice Jardine, *Gynesis: Configurations of Woman and Modernity* (Ithaca: Cornell University Press, 1985).

20 Derrida asserts that "Deconstruction, I have insisted, is not *neutral*. It *intervenes*." *Positions*, p. 93.

21 *Of Grammatology*, p. 9.

22 Ibid., p. 10.

23 Ibid., p. 9.

24 Ibid.

25 Derrida, *Margins*, p. 320.

26 Ibid., p. 310.

27 Michael Heim, in *Electric Language: A Philosophical Study of Word Processing* (New Haven: Yale University Press, 1987) similarly observes that "digital writing supplants the framework of the book: it replaces the craftsman's care for resistant materials with automated manipulation; deflects attention from personal expression toward the more general logic of algorithmic procedures; shifts the steadiness of the contemplative formulation of ideas into an over-abundance of dynamic possibilities; and turns the private solitude of reflective reading and writing into a public network where the personal symbolic framework

needed for original authorship is threatened by linkage with the total textuality of human expression" (p. 191).

28 See A. M. Turing, "Computing Machinery and Intelligence," *Mind*, 59 (236), October 1950, pp. 433–60, for a discussion of the test.

29 The typewriter may be thought to accomplish the same ends. Yet each typewriter leaves different markings on the page, as every fan of detective stories knows.

30 A writer can of course save a copy of each change or set of changes made to a file, thereby preserving a history of the composition of the work. I suspect this is rarely done or surely not with the relative completeness with which the manuscript preserves alterations.

31 The entire text was published by the Centre. See Jean-François Lyotard, *Les Immatériaux: Epreuves d'écritures* (Paris: Centre Georges Pompidou, 1985), p. 7. Also see the worthwhile review by John Rajchman: "The Postmodern Museum," *Art in America*, October 1985, pp. 111–17, 171.

32 *Les Immatériaux*, p. 19.

33 See Georg Simmel, *The Philosophy of Money*, trans. Tom Bottomore and David Frisby (London: Routledge and Kegan Paul, 1978) for an interpretation of the role of cities in identity formation.

34 Such anonymous subjectivity before the mode of information is found in personal ads in newspapers. While there is much playing with identity in these ads, they do not allow for extensive conversations. I am indebted to Renee Fraser for making the connection between personals and computer message services.

35 Message services are becoming increasingly common in the United States. One called Aline in New York is very successful and resembles the description below of the French minitel *messagier*. See James Bennet, "The Data Game," *The New Republic*, February 13, 1989, pp. 20–2.

36 For an interesting history of Minitel see Marie Marchant, *La Grande Aventure du Minitel* (Paris: Larousse, 1987). By 1988 there were about three million Minitels in use. See Steven Marcus, "The French Videotex Connection," *Issues in Science and Technology*, 4, Fall 1987, p. 108.

37 See Justine De Lacy, "The French Are Falling in Love With their Computers and Through Them," *New Yorker*, July 31, 1987. See also the special issue on the Minitel, "L'Année du

Minitel," *Le Nouvel Observateur*, 1156, January 2–8, 1987, pp. 40–7.

38 De Lacy, "The French," p. 92.

39 Marchand, *Grande Aventure*, p. 138.

40 Ibid., p. 74.

41 Ibid., p. 69.

42 Ibid., p. 144.

43 Ibid., p. 138.

44 Ibid., p. 93.

45 Ibid.

46 Starr Roxanne Hiltz and Murray Turoff, *The Network Nation: Human Communication via Computer* (London: Addison-Wesley, 1978), p. xxvi.

47 Jessie Bernard, *The Sociology of Community* (Glenview, Ill.: Scott-Foresman, 1973), p. 181.

48 Hiltz and Turoff, *Network Nation*, p. xxix.

49 For an excellent discussion and analysis of computer conferencing, see Andrew Feenberg, "Computer Conferencing and the Humanities," *Instructional Science*, 16, 1987, pp. 169–86.

50 Andrew Feenberg, "Moderating an Educational Teleconference," unpublished essay, has called attention to this feature of computer conferences.

51 Hiltz and Turoff, *Network Nation*, p. 105.

52 Ibid., p. 472.

53 Marc Guillaume refers to the new relation as "spectral." See Cathérine Bidou, Marc Guillaume and Véronique Prévost, *L'ordinaire de la télématique* (Paris: L'Iris, 1988).

54 Many of the features of electronic writing, especially of computer conferencing, might appear to conform to Habermas's counterfactual concept of "the ideal speech situation." Such an argument is made by Timothy Luke and Stephen K. White in "Critical Theory, the Information Revolution, and an Ecological Path to Modernity," in John Forester, ed., *Critical Theory and Public Life* (Cambridge, Mass.: MIT Press, 1985), pp. 22–53. Computer conferencing appears to remove, as Paul Rabinow suggested to me, asymmetrical contexts of speech acts thereby promoting the instanciation of "universal validity claims." Computer conferencing qualifies, in this view, as nondistorted communication, providing in principle free access to the public sphere while eliminating systems media such as money and power which are endemic distorting factors in "normal" communications situations in the lifeworld. While Habermasians

might want to pursue this line of thought, I think the deconstructionist perspective of a reconfiguration of self-constitution in electronic writing is a more fruitful line of analysis. For arguments sympathetic to Habermas's position see Peter Dews, *Logics of Disintegration: Post-Structuralist Thought and the Claims of Critical Theory* (London: Verso, 1987).

55   Jacques Derrida, *The Post Card: From Socrates to Freud and Beyond*, trans. Alan Bass (Chicago: University of Chicago Press, 1987), p. 5.

56   For an illuminating discussion of *The Post Card* see *Affranchissement du transfert et de la lettre* (Paris: Confrontation, 1982), especially the interventions by Derrida.

57   Sigmund Freud, *Civilization and Its Discontents* (New York: Norton, 1961), p. 39.

58   *The Post Card*, p. 44.

59   Ibid., p. 121.

60   Ibid., p. 404.

61   Ibid., p. 62.

62   Ibid., p. 103.

63   Ibid., p. 193.

64   Gregory Ulmer, "The Post-Age," *diacritics*, 11, 1981, p. 43.

65   *The Post Card*, pp. 104–5.

66   Ibid., p. 105.

67   See Stephen Kern, *The Culture of Time and Space: 1880–1918* (Cambridge, Mass.: Harvard University Press, 1983).

Chapter 5   Lyotard and Computer Science

1   Shoshana Zuboff, *In the Age of the Smart Machine: the Future of Work and Power* (New York: Basic Books, 1988), pp. 88–9.

2   Larry Hirschhorn, *The Workplace Within: Psychodynamics of Organizational Life* (Cambridge, Mass.: MIT Press, 1988).

3   Harry Braverman, *Labor and Monopoly Capital* (New York: Monthly Review Press, 1974), and David Noble, *Forces of Production: A Social History of Industrial Automation* (New York: Knopf, 1984).

4   For a discussion of the difficulties incurred by universities in their relation to corporations and to the government through new developments in natural science, see Jon Wiener, "Campus Capitalism: Harvard Chases Biotech Bucks," *The Nation*, January 2, 1989, pp. 12–16.

5   For an appreciation of the complexities of that period of science

see Frank E. Manuel, *A Portrait of Issac Newton* (Cambridge, Mass.: Harvard University Press, 1968).

6 See Bruno Latour, *Laboratory Life: The Social Construction of Scientific Facts* (Beverly Hills: Sage Publications, 1979) for a convincing social epistemology of the "lab".

7 Susan R. Bordo makes this argument in *The Flight to Objectivity: Essays on Cartesianism and Culture* (Stony Brook: State University of New York Press, 1987). See also Geof Bowker and Bruno Latour, "A Booming Discipline Short of Discipline: (Social) Studies of Science in France," *Social Studies of Science*, 17, 1987, pp. 715–48 for a discussion of various new directions in the sociology of scientific epistemology.

8 See for example Evelyn Fox Keller, *Reflections on Gender and Science* (New Haven: Yale University Press, 1985).

9 For instance Stanely Aronowitz, *Science as Power: Discourse and Ideology in Modern Society* (Minneapolis: University of Minnesota Press, 1988), and Joseph Rouse, *Knowledge and Power: Toward a Political Philosophy of Science* (Ithaca: Cornell University Press, 1987).

10 In *The Philosophical Discourse of Modernity*, trans. Frederick Lawrence (Boston: MIT Press, 1987) Habermas does not treat Lyotard. Manfred Frank made up for this lack in a series of lectures at University of California, Irvine, in March 1988 where he presented a Habermasian analysis of Lyotard in which he accused Lyotard of normless irrationalism and even, in the discussion, of promoting neofascism. See Rainer Rochlitz, "Des Philosophes allemands face à la pensée française: alternatives à la philosophie du sujet," *Critique*, 464–5, January/February 1986, pp. 7–39. Rochlitz, reviewing among others Manfred Frank's *What is Neostructuralism?*, argues against the poststructuralist multiplication of meaning on the pragmatic ground that in daily life one cannot exist by the principle of the "inexhaustible character of literary interpretation." For a more favorable view of the relation of poststructuralism to critical politics see Eve Tavor Bannet, *Structuralism and the Logic of Dissent: Barthes, Derrida, Foucault, Lacan* (Chicago: University of Illinois Press, 1989).

11 Michel Foucault, *Herculine Barbin, Being the Recently Discovered Memoirs of a Nineteenth-Century French Hermaphrodite*, trans. Richard McDougall (New York: Pantheon, 1980), French edition 1978.

12 Jürgen Habermas, *The Philosophical Discourse of Modernity* especially pp. 266-93.

13 "What is Enlightenment?," in Paul Rabinow, ed., *The Foucault Reader* (New York: Pantheon, 1984), pp. 32–50.

14 Gilles Deleuze and Félix Guattari, *A Thousand Plateaus: Capitalism and Schizophrenia*, trans. Brian Massumi (Minneapolis: University of Minnesota Press, 1987), p. 3.

15 Ibid., p. 492.

16 Ibid., p. 458.

17 Ernesto Laclau and Chantal Mouffe, *Hegemony and Socialist Strategy: Towards a Radical Democratic Politics*, trans. Winston Moore and Paul Cammack (London: Verso, 1985), pp. 152, 112.

18 Ibid., p. 113.

19 Ibid., p. 167.

20 Ibid., p. 4. For a Marxist critique of their position, along with their reply see Norman Geras, "Post-Marxism?," *New Left Review*, 163, May/June 1987, pp. 40–82, and Ernesto Laclau and Chantal Mouffe, "Post-Marxism without Apologies," *New Left Review*, 166, November/December, 1987, pp. 79–106.

21 Seminar at University of California, Irvine, April 20, 1989, entitled "Hegemonic Logics and Politics."

22 Laclau and Mouffe, *Hegemony and Socialist Strategy*, p. 107.

23 "Building a New Left: An Interview with Ernesto Laclau," *Strategies*, 1, Fall 1988, pp. 10–28.

24 Jean-François Lyotard, *The Postmodern Condition*, trans. Geoff Bennington and Brian Massumi (Minneapolis: University of Minnesota Press, 1984), p. xxiii.

25 John Kenneth Galbraith, *The New Industrial State* (New York: Signet, 1967).

26 Max Horkheimer and Theodor Adorno, *Dialectic of Enlightenment*, trans. John Cumming (New York: Seabury, 1972).

27 In the recent controversy over cold fusion, for example, computers have played an important but not necessarily salutory role in disseminating the initial research findings. Bulletin boards and computer conferences across the world debated the fusion experiment by Fleischmann and Pons, creating a new situation for scientists. See "Networks Can Hinder Research," *International Herald Tribune*, June 9, 1989, p. 13.

28 Evelyn Fox Keller, *Reflections on Gender and Science*, p. 64.

29 I decided to explore the discipline of Computer Science in relation to Lyotard's work and to the problem of science in the

mode of information. This field suggested itself because it is new and because of its obvious relation to the theme of the chapter. I am grateful to Leigh Star and Rob Kling for suggesting that I look at the Turing Award essays as a useful index of the way computer scientists define their field. For a nontechnical explanation of Turing's accomplishment see John Shore *The Sachertorte Algorithm and Other Antidotes to Computer Anxiety* (New York: Viking, 1985).

30 Jack Carlson, "On Determining Computer Science Education Programs," *Communications of the Association for Computing Machinery*, 9 (3), March 1966, p. 135.

31 Louis Fein, "ACM has a Crisis of Identity?," *Communications of the Association for Computing Machinery*, 10 (1), January 1967, p. 1.

32 Maurice Wilkes, "Computers Now and Then," *Journal of the Association for Computing Machinery*, 15 (1), January 1968, p. 7.

33 R. W. Hamming, "One Man's View of Computer Science," *Journal of the Association for Computing Machinery*, 16 (1), January 1969, p. 5.

34 Peter Denning, "Looking Back and Looking Ahead," *Communications of the Association for Computing Machinery*, 14 (12), December 1971, p. 820.

35 Allen Newell and Herbert A. Simon, "Computer Science as Empirical Inquiry: Symbols and Search," *Journal of the Association for Computing Machinery*, 19 (3), March 1976, p. 125.

36 John E. Hopcroft, "Computer Science: The Emergence of a Discipline," *Communications of the Association for Computing Machinery*, 30 (3), March 1987, p. 201.

37 For an argument for "weak" thinking see Gianni Vattimo, *The End of Modernity: Nihilism and Hermeneutics in Post-Modern Culture*, trans. John R. Synder (Cambridge: Polity Press, 1988).

38 Jean-François Lyotard and Jean-Loup Thébaud, *Just Gaming*, trans. Wlad Godzich (Minneapolis: University of Minnesota Press, 1985): "the regulating of dialogic discourse, even of dialectical discourse in the Platonic sense, seemed to me to be associated with power, since ultimately it aims at controlling the effects of the statements exchanged by the partners of the dialogue ..." (p. 4).

39 There is one place where Lyotard searches beyond the position of the philosopher for his discursive identity: "I do not believe

myself to be a philosopher, in the proper sense of the term, but a 'politician.'" Ibid., p. 55.

40 "One of the Things at Stake in Women's Struggles," trans. Deborah Clarke, Winifred Woodhull and John Mowitt, *Substance*, 20 (9), 1978, p. 13, from "Féminité dans la métalangue, " chapter 7 of *Rudiments païens: Genre dissertatif* (Paris: Union Générale d'Editions, 1977).

41 Page xiii, where Lyotard mocks the use of the prefix "post." The term "postmodern" is only used a few times in the book. On page 136 Lyotard asks, again mockingly, if postmodernity is "the passtime of an old man who scrounges in the garbageheap of finality looking for leftovers ... and who turns into the glory of his novelty . . .?" *The Differend: Phrases in Dispute*, trans. Georges Van Den Abbeele (Minneapolis: University of Minnesota Press, 1988). Original French edition, 1983.

42 Jean-François Lyotard, *Heidegger et "les juifs"* (Paris: Editions Galilee, 1988), p.45.

43 For a good discussion of the differend in relation to the unpresentable see Jean-François Lyotard, "Judiciousness in Dispute, or Kant After Marx," in Murray Krieger, ed., *The Aims of Representation: Subject/Text/History* (New York: Columbia University Press, 1987), pp. 23–68.

44 Paul de Man, *Wartime Journalism, 1939–1943*, ed. Werner Hamacher, Neil Hertz and Thomas Keenan (Lincoln: University of Nebraska Press, 1988).

45 Ken Anderson, Paul Piccone, Fred Siegel and Michael Taves, "Roundtable on Communitarianism" *Telos*, 76, Summer 1988, pp. 2–32.

46 *The Differend*, p. 162.

47 François Furet makes a great deal of what he calls the "new political sociability" invented during the years of the French Revolution. See *Interpreting the French Revolution*, trans. Elborg Foster (New York: Cambridge University Press, 1981), pp. 37, 173.

Names Index

178